THE SPECIAL PARENT'S HANDBOOK

by Yvonne Newbold

First published 2014 by Amity Books

ISBN: 978-1-910202-23-4

Printed in Great Britain for How2become Ltd by CMP (uk) Limited, Poole, Dorset.

For Francesca, Toby and Adam,
without a doubt the very best teachers I have ever had
I am so proud of all you have each overcome, and
what you have all achieved
As always, with all my love

Disclaimer

Although the author and publisher have made every effort to ensure that the information in this book was correct at press time, the author and publisher do not assume and hereby disclaim any liability to any party for any loss, damage, or disruption caused by errors or omissions, whether such errors or omissions result from negligence, accident, or any other cause. This book is not intended as a substitute for the medical advice of physicians. The reader should regularly consult a physician in matters relating to health, and particularly with respect to any symptoms that may require diagnosis or medical attention. The author accepts that this book is her own personal subjective opinion, and may not match recollections of others who were involved in the experiences described within. Some details may have been amended to preserve confidentiality and anonymity, and certain organisations such as hospitals, schools, local authorities and others are not named, since the purpose of this book is to focus on general experience of families rather than to focus on the particular practices in place at individual organisations.

Acknowledgements

There are so many people I would like to thank for their unwavering support while I have been writing this book over the past few months. In many respects it really has been a group effort.

A small handful of people read the early drafts of this book, and their support, encouragement, comments and really positive feedback has helped enormously, not just in being able to include some suggestions that I might not otherwise have thought of, but also because their belief in me and their enthusiasm for this project really kept me going all the way through. They are all experts in the subject matter of this book; not only do they include a doctor, a senior social worker, and an experienced teacher, but also three very "Special Parents", who really understand, because they, too, have children with disabilities.

Therefore, in strict alphabetical order, I would like to thank Dr Johnny Browne, Sian Cunningham, Hilary Lane, Linda Morbin, Petra Nelson, Benedicte Symcox and Heidi Thompson-Reed. They will never know how much I appreciate their input, and how their unstinting cheerleading in the background spurred me on to get the book finished.

I would also like to thank another very "Special Parent", who is also the mother of a daughter with disabilities, Rosa Monckton. Rosa took the time to not only to read it from cover to cover, but also to write the Foreword for this book. Her friendship and warm encouragement all the way through has been invaluable, too.

The recent photos on the cover were taken by Rachel Raphael, who made the photo session I'd been dreading great fun, very relaxed and a lovely afternoon. The photo of Toby when he was little was taken by Richard Bloomfield, who has very kindly given me permission to use what is one of my favourite ever photos of Toby. Thank you both.

Thanks must also go to Michael Darby, who did the clever techno stuff that converted Richard's lovely photo of Toby into a digital version so we could use it.

Richard McMunn, thank you for helping me make it happen, and holding my hand along every step of the publishing process.

Maurice Trimmer and Geraldine Trimmer, my father and my sister, have been there for me all the way through, just as they have been there, waiting in the wings and rushing forward to catch me whenever things got awkward, all the way through the children's childhoods. They also took the time to read the book and make very helpful suggestions, spotting typos and copy-editing the final version of the book. Thank you both, for everything.

Francesca and Adam have helped enormously, not just by allowing me to tell their stories, but by making useful suggestions, offering their continual support and encouragement, and by pointing out and correcting inaccuracies along the way. Toby was there all the way for me too, and although he doesn't understand that I have written a book, he was always ready to make me laugh when things were getting tough.

Last but by no means least, huge thanks have to go to Malcolm Cooper, the lovely man who believes in me, puts up with me and loves me, whatever crisis of confidence I put him through. He keeps me calm, makes me laugh, and makes the sun shine on even the rainiest and coldest days of our lives. His patience is endless. We aren't the easiest family in the world to take on, yet you have become such an important part of our family, that the children and I simply love you to bits. And he'll hate that I've written this, and no doubt he'll cringe because he'll think it's cheesy. If you've ever read my blog, Malcolm is the real WM, the wonderful man who made all the difference.

CONTENTS

Foreword by Rosa Monckton 8

Introduction 10

Chapter 1 – Getting the bad news 14

Chapter 2 – He said....she said 33

Chapter 3 – The Advancing Army of Professionals 44

Chapter 4 – When the dust starts to settle 61

Chapter 5 – Building your support network 77

Chapter 6 – Your child 88

Chapter 7 – Siblings 99

Chapter 8 – Becoming the Expert 119

Chapter 9 – Being in Hospital 137

Chapter 10 – Hospital Appointments 160

Chapter 11 – Intensive Care 176

Chapter 12 – CAMHS 189

Chapter 13 – Education 197

Chapter 14 – Social Services 219

Chapter 15 – Food Issues 229

Chapter 16 – Meltdowns 241

Chapter 17 – And Finally 248

Foreword

Reading Yvonne's searing, honest and raw account of bringing up her children left me almost speechless with anger. Anger at all that she has had to go through in order to get the best possible life for them; anger at the way she has been treated; anger in the face of the numerous, pointless meetings she has had to attend, with the mindless, meaningless jargon; and above all, anger at the total lack of commonsense and compassion shown to her family.

What sort of a society do we want to live in? Surely it is one where its weakest and most vulnerable members are properly looked after, and protected. A society where a mother who is bringing up three disabled children on her own is given all the support that is required, without question.

Yvonne writes her family's life story without a trace of self-pity, indeed it is the factual detailing of her day to day existence which is so heartbreaking. From the moment of her son Toby's diagnosis, when a doctor "bounded into our room beaming all over her face", to being sent home after a two minute lesson on tube-feeding to start her new life of 'round the clock two hourly tube feeding night and day, with no-one asking if I was OK.'

She is nakedly honest about the moments when it seemed impossible to cope. The depths of despair that you face in the middle of yet another sleepless night are so profound, so all encompassing, that the idea of the ultimate blackness seems welcome. Yet there are moments of humour too, and a stoical acceptance of what life has thrown her way. Throughout it all there is a tremendous pride in all that her children have achieved, against overwhelming odds. What is not said, but which leaps off every page, is that Yvonne is an extraordinary and exemplary mother, juggling with the needs of her three children without ever considering her own. She is a shining beacon of motherhood, and this book is all the more powerful as a result.

It is an important book to have written, and will be a lifeline to any parent of a disabled child. However, it should also be read by all professionals who have anything to do with people who have a disability. Yvonne has written not just a story of her family, but a story of our time. We should all be ashamed of what we have become, and ask ourselves why, as a society, we are so lacking in humanity.

Rosa Monckton

Introduction

When my son Toby was born with multiple disabilities and complex medical needs, I was plunged into a completely new world which was both frightening and isolating. There was no rule-book, no set of instructions, no-one I knew who had ever shared this strange and scary new world.

I have tried to write the book I wish someone had been able to give me that day; a book that would have told me that others have been there, a book that would have given me hope that I could get through this if I trusted my instincts and allowed my brand new little baby boy to lead us both where we needed to go. I had to learn things the hard way, and what I couldn't learn I had to make up as I went along.

We've done OK, even though, later in childhood, both Toby's brother and sister, Adam and Francesca, would also be diagnosed with disorders, conditions and disabilities entirely unrelated to the ones that Toby has. Actually, we've done a lot better than simply OK, we've had a lot of fun on the way through childhood, pulled together as a family, made a load of very good friends and my children are now emerging into adulthood as confident, happy and talented young people with a huge amount to offer the world.

We took it a day at a time, we remembered to laugh every day, and even on the worst of days we tried to find the nice things that happened too. It wasn't always easy, but neither was it as difficult as I had feared.

This book is partly a parenting handbook, sharing some of the lessons I've learnt along the way, partly the story of our family growing up, and partly me highlighting some of the frustrations and annoyances that parents of children like ours have to endure, often needlessly, because the very services created to help children like ours often create unnecessary stress, exhaustion and misery, and hinder more than they help.

It's not always like that. You will also meet people along the way who are willing to work hard to transform your lives, who will listen and truly care, and you will never forget their kindnesses. You will also make some very good friends, friends who will always be there for you no matter what.

I didn't always do it well, in fact I made some clangers of mistakes, and led myself and my family up some pretty blind alleys sometimes. That's when we all learn the best lessons in life.

Disability comes in all shapes and sizes, and my children are proof of this. Toby's disabilities are obvious and very complex, whilst Francesca and Adam have disabilities that are virtually invisible. People look at Toby and can see how severely his disabilities affect him. Francesca and Adam, in some ways have had it much harder, because their disabilities have often gone unrecognised. They are both intelligent, articulate and considerate, and often there was absolutely no indication whatsoever that anything was amiss. If only people knew how tough things often really were for both of them, and how hard it has been to access the right sort of help along the way. People think disability means being in a wheelchair, but it is so much more than that.

Some people prefer to use words other than disability, the terms "special needs" or "additional needs" or "impairment" somehow seem kinder and more socially acceptable. I'm not sure it does our children any favours, in fact I think it actively short-changes them by understating their very real difficulties. Parents already struggle to unlock budgets and funding from the Statutory Services for our children with disabilities. Funding for vital services and equipment that are essential for our children's development and well-being. One of the most common, and often the most undermining way in which the professionals manage to deny our children this funding is to minimise their difficulties and therefore reduce the perception of need. For parents like us to use euphemisms ourselves that also minimise our children's needs seems to me like scoring an own goal.

It has been quite a responsibility writing a book that may thrust my children into the public domain, and it's been a subject of much debate in our household too, with the occasional crisis of confidence along the way. Unfortunately, Toby hasn't the mental capacity to understand anything about this task that I have undertaken, although Francesca and Adam are both very supportive and have been very generous in allowing me to tell their stories. It's been an interesting time because my recollection of events has often been different from theirs, and together we have had some interesting discussions about what is and is not permissible to reveal. We came to a family decision that anything that happened to Francesca or Adam before the age of eleven was completely acceptable for me to write about; any events which occurred when they were older have only been included with their individual express permission.

This book is primarily for parents, but I am hopeful that health, education and social care professionals may also find it useful.

The book covers the initial stages of shock when your child is first diagnosed, through the slow process of coming to terms with the new challenges facing your family, how you become the true expert of your child's condition, how to create some semblance of ordinary family life, coping with the endless meetings that begin to dominate your life, and the three areas of statutory services that will delight and dismay you in equal measures, the NHS, Education and Social Services. I've also included a chapter on each of two of the most common difficulties that face families like ours, Food Issues and Meltdowns, passing on some of the tried and tested strategies we've developed along the way.

During Toby's childhood there have been major shifts in the way the Statutory Services interface with families like ours. The most promising one, in my view, is the move toward Partnership Working, where parents are acknowledged as being key players in decisions about their children. I've watched this shift develop and grow in some areas such as social services, and be marginalised and ignored in others, the NHS in particular with Education not that far behind. I hope that by the time the next generation of our children reach adulthood it will be universally recognised that involving parents in decisions is the approach that achieves the very best outcomes for our children, and will be implemented and working well across all three sectors.

I don't know whether I've achieved what I set out to do. The hardest part of writing this book was having to decide what to include and what to leave out. I could have written a whole book or maybe several on just about every chapter.

There are likely to be other books in the pipeline, but a lot depends on my health. I was diagnosed with bi-lateral breast cancer in May 2012, and nearly a year later, despite intensive cancer treatment, it was also found in my spine which means it is now incurable. However I am receiving continuing treatment, and I'm relatively stable at the moment, but my long-term prognosis isn't as great as I'd like it to be.

The things I have learnt in bringing up my children have helped me enormously in taking my diagnosis in my stride. Things like living in the moment, not worrying too much about tomorrow, and believing that, however bleak things may seem today, they can only get better.

It's also been the wake-up call I needed to get going and write the book I've always threatened to write. There's nothing quite like incurable cancer to make you realise that there's no time like the present!

If you enjoy this book, you can visit "The Special Parent's Handbook" page on Facebook and my website, www.yvonnenewbold.com to see what's planned next. It is always lovely hearing from people, so please leave a comment to say hello if you feel like it.

Thank you so much for reading

Yvonne Newbold

CHAPTER 1
Getting the Bad News

Sitting opposite a doctor while they tell you your child has some form of lifelong illness, condition, additional need or disability is never going to be easy. These moments will live with us for the rest of our lives, defining us and changing the landscape of our families forever.

There is no going back; no being able to scoop all this awful news up off the floor and pack it away where it can't hurt anybody. It's there, laid out in front of you, and it is hurting like hell. Bad news affects us all differently, and we will all react in different ways. The shock may make the room spin, or seem like everything is unfolding in slow motion, or make you feel sick, or make you want to run away screaming into the woods. It's fairly likely that right now, you won't be able to take in everything you're being told either.

This doctor has just said a series of words which changes everything for the rest of your life. These words are ones that no parent ever wants to have to hear. You probably believe, like we all did once, that these things are something that only happens to "other people". You are now in that "other people" club, a club you never ever wanted to join.

Right now, you will feel you can't possibly cope, but I promise you, you will surprise yourself and cope magnificently well. Not straight away, and not every day, but over time you will learn to dig deep into yourself and find resources you never knew were there. We all do.

One of the hardest things is that often there isn't time to process your own feelings, because actually, this hasn't happened to you, it's happened to your child. It's your job as their parent to hold them close, support them, love them and find a way to help them grow and develop into a confident and happy young person who can find their own place in the world, because disability or not, this is still their world, and their one shot at life, and they deserve the very best of it, just as you do too.

It's not going to be easy. There will be days when you will just want to rant and rail at the unfairness in the world and start doubting that you can do this at all. You can.

It's not all bad though. Your child will bring out the best in you and other people around you. Your child will make you laugh and make you love like you didn't know you were capable of loving and laughing before. They will teach you things that most people would never imagine exist, they will introduce you to all sorts of new experiences and some really lovely people too. They will help you to see what really matters in life and what doesn't, and most of all, they will make you become the very best person you ever could be.

You won't see any of that on the day you get the diagnosis, though. All you'll see is confusion, heartbreak and devastation ahead, with the world falling in for good measure, too. We were all there, and that's totally normal. Nobody learns anything that's worth learning in an instant, and you won't have a clue how to parent a disabled child right now. That's fine, you'll learn as you go along, and you've been given the best teacher in the world to help you get there – your own child.

These diagnosis-moments come in all shapes and sizes, sometimes before your baby is even born, sometimes at birth or weeks or even years later. Sometimes a proper, formal diagnosis of a known and named condition never comes at all, even though your child is desperately ill and severely disabled. My son, Toby, falls into this category; we've had a whole string of mini-diagnoses about each of his symptoms, but with no name to an overall condition because he is completely unique. He, like many others up and down the country, are known as SWAN children, which stands for Syndromes Without a Name.

Sometimes the news is delivered with an appropriate degree of compassion and sensitivity, and sometimes it simply isn't. It may come as a bolt-out-of-the-blue totally unexpected shock, or it may actually carry some element of relief following harrowing periods of worry, tests and procedures to find out what's wrong.

However it happens, it completely floors you. I know, I've been there, not once, but on three separate occasions with each of my three children. Each time it was completely different on lots of different levels, the ages of the children, the way in which the news was delivered and my own personal reaction to each of the situations. There are no rights or wrongs, no "proper" way to react, you just have to take it on the chin and roll in whatever direction the punches take you, before you can get up again and start to learn how to deal with it.

You won't just learn to deal with it, in time you'll become a really special parent, discovering strengths you never knew you had, and developing new ones on the way, too.

Toby's Story

Toby is my second child, born when my daughter, Francesca, was eighteen months old. The moment he was born I knew immediately that something was very wrong indeed. He was 2 weeks late, but had premature characteristics such as a very low birth-weight and downy hair all over him. Most of all, he looked as if his skin was several sizes too big for his body, all wrinkled in folds like no baby I'd ever seen before. Maybe it was a sixth sense, but I just knew.

He was the only one of my three who mastered breast-feeding like he was a pro. I'd had a nightmare time trying to establish breast-feeding with Francesca, and after weeks of tears, trials and tribulations, as well as a hired electric breast-pump that made me feel like a cow only far less cute, I was totally thrilled that Toby could breastfeed, and was incredibly proud of both of us.

As they say, pride comes before a fall, and many weeks later they were to find my breast-milk had entered his lungs and that I had nearly drowned him.

However, despite his low birth-weight and peculiar looks, the maternity ward used this breast-feeding success as the basis to confirm that he was doing well, and therefore, was thought to be healthy enough to come home with me the following morning.

Every time I fed him, he turned blue, his breathing became laboured or stopped for a second or two, and his face looked like he was in extreme pain. I talked to everyone I could think of about it, but got reassurance from two different GPs, a Health Visitor and the Midwives on several occasions. I badgered them so much about my fears that my GP and Health Visitor began to think I was developing post-natal depression and was perhaps feeling some sort of "feeding-guilt" because Toby was able to breastfeed when I had failed dismally with Francesca.

I began to doubt myself instead of advocating for Toby. After all, I had no reason to question my total faith in the medical profession. Yes, on bad days, I still beat myself up over that one.

The niggling worry wouldn't go away though. I started making all sorts of excuses to pop into the doctor's surgery for one reason or another, until one day, when Toby was 2 weeks old, I saw a different GP, a locum.

He took one look at Toby and promptly called an ambulance, and started CPR until it arrived. Scary scary stuff, and yet on one level, I could feel the relief flooding right through me too.

So Toby was admitted to hospital, they inserted a naso-gastric tube, and put him on all sorts of treatments and therapies. A couple of weeks later, the NG (naso-gastric) tube was removed, Toby seemed better, and we went home, where, within 24 hours, all the same breathing problems and my worries started all over again. This started a pattern of regular hospital admissions - 4 days at home where he would get progressively more poorly, followed by an admission to hospital where they would make him better and send him home well, and then under my care he would get poorly all over again.

I was an intelligent, assertive, loving and attentive mother in my early thirties, with a successful management career behind me, but I began to think it must be all my fault. He would do well in hospital, then he would come home and get ill again. What on earth was I doing that was so wrong?

The one big difference between him being in hospital or being at home was that in hospital, they always inserted a naso-gastric tube, removing it on the morning he would be discharged. Of course on many occasions, I'd discussed with the hospital doctors my very real fears that he wasn't swallowing properly in some way, and that maybe my breast-milk was going into his lungs, but they kept reassuring me that that wasn't really possible and couldn't happen with the pattern of symptoms he was exhibiting.

Chest infection followed chest infection, serious ones with collapsed lungs, transfers to the Paediatric Intensive Therapy Unit (ITU) where he was often put on a ventilator. Watching him hovering between life and death became a fairly normal occurrence, and both we and his medical team knew we were on a race to find out what was going wrong before whatever it was killed him. Meanwhile, I was getting paranoid, convinced they would start to think it must be all my fault. I even started asking myself, could it be me? Might I have some terrible form of mental illness where I was harming my own baby without knowing or remembering?

I never left his side, either in hospital or at home, trying to stay awake all night when he was home just watching him sleep to make sure he was safe and breathing normally. Breathing normally? It just never happened, he had begun to develop a pattern where he would just stop breathing altogether, completely at random, something he would continue to do for the next ten years. When he was in hospital, I stayed on a camp bed by his side all night, and during the day, my husband would drop Francesca off at the hospital on his way to work, so very early, before she arrived, I would create a playpen fun area under his cot for her with paint pots and jigsaws and play-dough to keep her occupied and happy during our endless long days cooped up altogether in a side room on the hospital ward. During these weeks, we were transferred to other hospitals for further tests too, days on end where I had to leave Francesca with family and friends while Toby and I were miles away from home.

All the time, I was just waiting for that "Eureka" moment where they'd find out what was wrong, put it right and make him completely better. It simply hadn't occurred to me that doctors couldn't always perform such magic.

One day, a fairly normal day in the new pattern of our lives, Toby, Francesca, myself and their dad on a lunchtime visit, were all confined together in the airless, tiny side room which was, by now, our second home, when a doctor bounded in, beaming all over her face and unable to contain her excitement. "We've found it", she said. "He's got Pseudo-Bulbar Palsy!"

She went on to explain that this means his throat doesn't co-ordinate properly, that any matter, even his own saliva, has a good chance of entering his lungs instead of his stomach. Basically, exactly what I had been talking about to the doctors for weeks as to what I thought was happening, the very suggestion they had dismissed time and again as not possible medically, given the overall presenting picture of symptoms.

This young doctor was so thrilled, that I stupidly thought this was fabulous news. "So, what can you do to make it work properly?" I asked. Still grinning from ear to ear, pleased that she had finally been able to give us an explanation for his long-term difficulties, she said "Nothing!". Then she proceeded to add on, just as a little bonus, that this almost certainly meant he would have some form of life-long disability too, just for good measure.

I look back now and marvel at my naivete. I knew my baby boy was desperately ill, with some life-threatening medical condition, but disabled? The thought had never even occurred to me.

The doctor was still chattering away, saying that the plan was to teach me how to tube feed him, BISH BASH BOSH job done, and then to send me home with a baby who definitely had a broken throat, but also some unknown type of disability too.

I was exhausted from months of trying to hold it all together on virtually no sleep, with two tiny children, and a fractured life-style spread between home and countless different hospitals. We all have a tipping point when we just can't take anymore, and this young, smiley doctor had just found mine.

I opened my mouth and a scream came out, longer and louder than I thought it possible to scream, and I thought it was going to last forever. I pushed past her and ran away, as far as I could get, through the traffic on the main road, onto a park and just kept on running and running, trying, I think, to get as far away from the horror of this unfolding situation as I possibly could. In a wooded area I finally stopped, slumped to the ground by a tree and I howled like a baby for what must have been at least a couple of hours. Eventually a hospital porter found me and led me back to the ward, where my then husband, Chris, had packed up all our belongings and was holding Toby, now dressed and ready to come home.

Nobody mentioned my outburst or my running away. A jolly nurse was waiting to give me a two minute very basic lesson on tube-feeding, then that was that, we then got in the car with our newly disabled baby and his big sister, to start our new life of round-the-clock two-hourly tube-feeding, night and day, with no one even asking if I was OK.

Francesca's Story

Francesca wasn't diagnosed until she was nine. Ever since she was a baby, she had a funny little wriggly movement she did with her hands. Of course, taking her to the doctor didn't work, because she never did it during the 10 minute appointment time. She would get checked over, I would be told she was fine, and if there was any little habit going on, just to ignore it and she would grow out of it.

She didn't. She was five when we were living at Guy's Hospital, and I had noticed that these movements increased at times of stress, or at times of extreme excitement or happiness. During our months there, outwardly she was a very happy, engaging little girl, but these movements had increased so that she was doing it virtually constantly, and some of Toby's medical team became concerned about it too. It did seem to be stress-related to some degree, and there was certainly a lot of stress going on in the family at the time, with a very ill child in intensive care, but stress wasn't the whole picture by any means; even when she was very relaxed it would reduce in frequency, but not disappear entirely.

Francesca was referred for some tests, and a psychologist wanted to know how often this movement of hers was happening. However, they were too frequent to count as they actually happened, so Francesca was given free access to a lovely playroom with a hidden camera, and was filmed as she played. After the session, the video was slowed down and her wriggly movements were counted. Even when she was relaxed, content and totally absorbed in play, she was repeating her wriggly arm movement up to 40 times in a single minute.

They thought she may have some form of epilepsy, but when the tests came back negative, they formed the hypothesis that it was entirely stress-related and was caused by the edge-of-seat unpredictability of Toby's condition, and the related stress it was causing within the family. I told them she had been doing it since she was three months old, more than a year before Toby was born, but they didn't really take that on board. I was advised never to mention or draw attention to the problem, and to also ensure that everyone in her circle, including school, also knew to totally ignore it, and that, in time, it would eventually disappear.

It didn't. Francesca had to cope with some difficult episodes of bullying, mimicking and taunting all the way through primary school, and she had nowhere to take her worries about her funny wriggle because everyone was under strict instructions never to talk about it. If she brought the subject up, I would give her a hug, tell her not to worry about it, and that everyone had something a bit different about themselves. Generally, though, we coped reasonably well, she had some good friends at school too, and we muddled along.

One evening, she came to me once her two little brothers were in bed, and very earnestly asked me all about it, and asked if I could find out why she did it. So I took a deep breath and we went onto Dr Google, and tried to find out. Again and again, whatever keyword I entered, the same result would bounce back at us, "Tourette's Syndrome". I was sitting at the computer screen with my beautiful, clever, talented, caring, lovely young daughter beside me, trying to stay upbeat and cheerful whilst inwardly I could feel that my heart and my breathing had seized up completely in fear. "What's Tourette's Syndrome, Mummy?", she asked. I lied. "I don't know, darling, but hey, we'll go to the doctor and find out".

I remained secretly distraught for quite some time, holding it together until past her bedtime every night when I would just collapse into a heap of blubbing misery, convinced she was going to hit adulthood regarded as some type of freak, isolated and ridiculed and desperately unhappy. I just couldn't see any hope on the horizon at all.

So we went off to our doctor, who referred us to a Paediatrician, who referred us to a specialist Neurological Team, and meanwhile I read everything I could find out about Tourette's Syndrome.

By now the diagnosis seemed inevitable, and I knew what was coming, once Francesca had had a whole morning of tests and assessments. The Professor we saw could not have been kinder, more sensitive and genuinely compassionate as she confirmed my fears, that yes, Francesca did have Tourette's Syndrome.

The Professor had this lovely way of getting both parent and child on side, and she radiated with warmth, empathy and a really positive attitude. By this point, I was just feeling a bit sad, but resigned, and fairly knowledgeable about what Tourette's actually was. Francesca, though, was just so happy she was beaming so widely that I thought her face would split in two. At the time it seemed to me that Francesca was thrilled to have a name for her condition, and was feeling proud and pleased to know that she was one of many in this newly discovered very special group of people, a sort of exclusive Tourette's Syndrome club of people all over the world.

It helped that the Professor gave us both all sorts of really positive information, some names of famous people who also had Tourette's, books to read, associations to join; all sorts of interesting, useful and very positive stuff.

There was one big surprise though that day at the hospital out-patient's clinic. The most noticeable of Francesca's symptoms, the repetitive movement that had initiated my internet research which, in turn, had led us to this Tourette's Syndrome clinic appointment, wasn't Tourette's Syndrome at all. It was a completely unrelated condition, and was called a Stereotypy. Her Tourette's was diagnosed by a whole team of professionals in the room watching her throughout the morning, and surreptiously recording any tics, either vocal or motor ones, that she had demonstrated. They counted the number of different tics, the severity, the type and the repetitive nature of each separate one. I thought every child fidgeted and made odd little vocal sounds. They do, but Francesca's were way out beyond normal ranges and that's why she was diagnosed with Tourette's Syndrome, not because of the one very obvious repetitive movement that she had had since she was 3 months old.

The professor had never before seen a child who presented with both Tourette's Syndrome and a Stereotopy, the two are normally never linked. So, in her own way, Francesca was as unique as Toby.

Adam's Story

So I still had one "neuro-typical" child left, Adam. "Mummy, when am I going to be disabled too?" No, darling, you don't want to be disabled. "But Mummy I do, I really do because then I could go to Mencap and play with all their amazing toys, like Toby does". They say you should be careful about what you wish for.

Adam's diagnosis was actually hilarious, if you can have such a thing. Over the years I'd had several chats with him along the lines of "But mummy, I am disabled, too". It was a bit of an in-joke, that you only felt normal in our family if you weren't type of thing, but it was very cute.

When Adam was 8, Francesca wanted to go to a Tourette's Syndrome Conference being held in Central London, an all day-long meeting that was going to finish in the early evening. I managed to get Toby into respite, but couldn't get babysitting cover for Adam, so both he and Francesca were allowed to miss school and we all went up together.

It was a fantastic day. There were lots of children around Adam's age, and a whole programme of activities organised for them to run concurrently with the adult conference. Adam had a load of fun playing with other little boys, and one of the highlights of the day for him was when a musician with Tourette's Syndrome sat with him at the piano on stage and taught him to play the Simpson's signature tune. A lot of the children he was playing with had also been diagnosed with Tourettes, and he was fully occupied and engaged while Francesca, being considerably older, sat with me in the main conference room listening to the speakers and learning more about her condition.

The guest star was Pete from Big Brother, who also has Tourette's, and he had won that year's Big Brother. He was fabulous with both my kids, and we still have photos of them with him. Mostly, though, Adam was off doing his own thing with the smaller children, and having an absolute ball.

At one point during the afternoon Adam broke away from the other children, and came over to find me in the main room, while we were listening to the speakers. In a loud stage-whisper, he said "Mummy, now I know I'm right, I am disabled, I've got Tourette's too". "No, Adam, you don't, don't be silly", I whispered back, and he went off, I thought to play with the other kids.

Then I saw him. He was walking purposefully towards the podium, where Francesca's favourite Professor was standing, very luckily at that moment not actually addressing the audience, thank goodness. We were in auditorium-type seating, and even though I tried to, there was no way I could get there first and intercept him. When I finally caught up with him, the Professor was bent right down at his level, and they were having a very earnest chat. "Oh hello, Mummy, I've just been telling the Professor that I have Tourette's too just like Francesca, and she believes me even if you don't". There are moments when you just want the ground to open up and swallow you in as quickly as possible.

The Professor and I both knew that her clinic was so over-subscribed that getting an appointment with her would be virtually impossible, so, treating him with every bit as much importance and respect as she had always given Francesca, she said, "Adam, next time your sister comes to see me in clinic, I'd feel really honoured if you could come too, as my very special guest". I just love that lady.

Of course Adam was diagnosed with Tourette's too. As well as being diagnosed with everything Francesca had been diagnosed with, it turned out he had a whole load of extra bonus conditions as well. How on earth had I not noticed? Once they were all spelt out it was so flipping obvious I couldn't believe that it had passed me by. It was perhaps that he and his sisters' conditions present very differently, so I didn't recognise them, or perhaps it was because we have had to develop a different way of looking at things in our family, so that some things that are blindingly obvious to others just don't sink in with us.

Both Francesca and Adam have diagnoses that may well seem catastrophic in somebody else's family, but next to Toby's difficulties they sometimes hardly register at all. In a lot of ways, I think they have benefitted from this approach. Compared to Toby, they barely see themselves as disabled, and I think that has given them both a much more healthy perspective on their problems.

Adam's Earlier Story

When I was pregnant with Adam, because Toby had been diagnosed with such an obscurely severe condition, I was offered every pre-natal test on the planet, and then some.

The Obstetrician met with both Chris and me at 20 weeks, and dropped the bombshell; it was highly likely our baby was even more profoundly disabled than Toby, because not only did it seem probable that he shared Toby's difficulties, but that he also had Down's Syndrome. I was offered a termination either immediately or, due to the extreme circumstances, any time up to 38 weeks.

It was horrific. Shock and disbelief all over again, but I just knew that, whatever happened, I was keeping this baby. I'd already had 5 miscarriages, including one late-term one. With a history like that, you don't terminate lightly. However, I also knew that I was stretched to my limits coping with Toby's care, and that a second baby with similar issues could easily push our family over the edge.

I held onto the word "probable"; they definitely hadn't said definitely. I knew as well that if I was to terminate because this child might be born like Toby, it would be as if I was rejecting Toby too. I just knew I couldn't do that.

However, my husband took the opposite viewpoint, as did many members of my friends and family. I felt very pressured and unsupported, and whereas pregnancy should be a really happy and hopeful time, I can only remember the arguments, the tears and the unhappiness, as well as the complete fear of what the future might hold, knowing full well that many of the people who had been so supportive since Toby had been born three years previously, were appalled at what they saw as my utter stupidity in insisting on continuing with this pregnancy.

When I went into labour, we had a whole team of obstetricians as well as a full team of paediatricians on standby, including Toby's main Consultant, even though Adam made his grand entrance into the world at 2am in the morning.

The second I saw him I just knew he was fine. He was the image of Francesca, healthy, robust and with a fierce intelligence already evident at less than a minute old. It broke my heart that they took him from me for nearly an hour to run every possible test on him to make sure he was OK. It had to be done, even though I still hate to think what long-term effect such trauma in a baby's first hour may have had.

The flip-side of ante-natal screening

Adam and I were very lucky, but many parents are faced with the termination dilemma if an abnormality is suspected during pregnancy. The decision is an enormously difficult one, and I faced a level of open hostility and vocal contempt when I made my choice consistently clear. Every time I look at Adam I am so pleased I stuck to my guns, he is growing up to be such a lovely young man with so many talents and opportunities.

However, sticking to my guns was hard when I was faced with almost universal opposition. There seems to be a widespread cultural expectation that a negative scan result should always end in termination, which makes it very hard on parents who, for whatever reason, decide to continue with the pregnancy. These parents still have to cope with the same degree of shock, sadness and sense of loss common to all parents in a similar situation, but additionally they have to rise above a powerfully strong climate of disapproval, with many people openly expressing their own feelings that they have done the wrong thing and are making a mistake.

It is only the parents themselves who can know how they feel about such a personal matter, and find a way forward that is right for them. They are having to make one of the most, if not the most, difficult decision of their whole lives. They need time and space to find the best thing to do in their own unique circumstances, and regardless of what their final decision is, ideally they should get the love and support of their family and friends, rather than unsolicited advice and censure.

Reeling with shock

There is nothing that can take away the multi-layered pain that a diagnosis of your child's disability will bring. There really aren't adequate words to describe how awful it feels, like being hit simultaneously 6 times by trucks coming from different directions while falling over a cliff and being in a burning building, only a thousand times worse. Most parents would give their own limbs to make it not be so, yet there is absolutely nothing we can do to change it.

Parents often have a strong, almost primal, belief that they ought to be able to protect their children and keep them safe from any harm, or at the very least, make them feel better when things go wrong. There really isn't a more brutal way to find out that not everything can be sorted out with a cuddle and a sticking-plaster.

However, the way we are told the news has a huge impact, and although it may not lessen the pain at the time, it can help later on in laying the foundations for parents to accept the unacceptable in a much more constructive way.

The Professor was simply brilliant at it. Both children left her room feeling good about themselves, and perfectly happy about having Tourettes. It was great that both children were so happy, and each time we left the consulting room armed with a reading list and a lot of information about the condition, all presented in a really positive way.

The doctor who had burst into the room to tell me about Toby didn't mean to, but I doubt she could have handled it any worse. She was in a very different emotional place to where I was. She was approaching it from a scientific point of view, and for her, finally finding a missing piece to the jigsaw puzzle was enormously exciting and she couldn't wait to share it with me. She seemed very young and inexperienced, and perhaps too immature to be the one to tell me. While to her it was exciting, to me it was probably the most devastating piece of news a parent could hear. Your child is unlikely to eat or drink normally, he may never talk, he probably has disabilities too, but hey ho isn't that fabulous and look, I can't stop bouncing up and down and beaming about it. We were in different places, that's all, but I couldn't see it so simply then. That was the day I fell completely over the edge, and it took a very long time to climb back again.

However it is that we hear the unthinkable news, we are going to feel completely overwhelmed with bewilderment and deep sorrow, but I think there are many factors that can help shorten the length of time during which we feel so lost and unsettled. The first of these factors is the level of compassion, sensitivity and understanding with which the news is delivered.

There was nothing positive at all in the way Toby's news was presented. There is always a positive, even if it's only "well at least we know now". Looking back, there were several obvious positive things that could have been said – "it means that you can take him home today once you are confident about tube-feeding", or "we now know what's been causing his breathing problems and chest infections, we can build on that", or any one of a dozen others. Or the negatives could have been minimised. It was probably too much to expect me, there and then, to take on board that he was also likely to have disabilities. He was only 3 months old; that news could have waited until another day.

Reading lists, information, support groups, charities or associations specialising in aspects of the condition help enormously too. When I got home nursing Toby's news, I had nothing to hold on to, so my mind and my imagination went into overdrive. It really helps if you can find something to read, someone to talk to, and somewhere to find out more information, even if you can't face absorbing any of it just yet. Knowing that you can refer to something if you need to is very reassuring indeed.

It may feel as if everything about the world you ever knew has come crashing down around you, and you are likely to be in a very shocked state, which may continue for quite some time. More than ever, it is so important to take care of yourself.

The depths of despair you may feel can make it seem as if you are sinking into some form of madness, but it will pass; it's the fear, worry and shock that are causing it. Go with your feelings, let them wash over you, weep buckets if you need to. It won't last forever, you will come through this and out the other side when your mind has had time to take in and process everything you're having to take on board right now.

This is when you may need help, because you may not be able to function properly, Call on family, friends and neighbours, people rally round and help in a way you would never think possible in the days following such awful news.

I'd never even been inside our local church, but someone told them about Toby's diagnosis and I was overwhelmed by the kindness people from this church extended towards us. Complete strangers would knock on our door with a fully cooked meal, offers to do shopping, and even to help look after Francesca, or to take her out for an afternoon.

In very rare cases, parents really can find themselves struggling emotionally, and it's not uncommon for such parents to start self-medicating with alcohol or drugs, or to experience moments of such lows that they start thinking of self-harming or suicide. If you are in any way concerned about yourself, or anyone you know in this situation, please get urgent help, either from your GP, or if the situation is particularly acute, you can call an ambulance. These cases are extremely uncommon, but they do affect a very small minority of parents, and it's always better to be safe than sorry; to call for expert help sooner rather than later.

TIPS, TRICKS AND STRATEGIES

If at all possible, make sure you have someone with you for any medical "bad news" moments.

Ask for help – get a friend to pull together support for you for the next few days. You're in shock, you can't do the small stuff right now, like shopping, cooking or bathing the kids.

Look after yourself – sleep, eat and drink enough fluids.

Expect to feel like pants. It will pass but just go with it, scream, cry, howl, withdraw, whatever feels cathartic, just do it and wallow for now without beating yourself up over it. Better out than in.

Do you have enough information about your child's condition, and do you feel up to reading it all yet? There may come a moment when you suddenly need to know everything there is to know about your child's condition, and when that moment comes you'll want to have as much information as possible at your fingertips.

Often, shock prevents parents taking everything in when they are first given the news about their child's disability or illness. Even if they do, later there will be new questions they have about their child's condition.

It can be very helpful to ring the hospital and ask for another appointment with the same Consultant a few weeks down the line to talk things through again, once you are in a clearer frame of mind.

Delegate and offload. Anything and everything, or even better, find someone who can delegate everything for you.

If it helps, keep a notepad close and jot down your random thoughts, you'll never remember them otherwise. These thoughts can form the basis of questions for when you next see the medical team, or they may be intuitive thoughts that, when added together, help you to find coping solutions and ideas.

Friends, family and acquaintances will be very concerned about you, and will want to know everything as and when it happens. Right now you are not strong enough to repeat all this awfulness time and time again to keep everyone in the loop. Having the same difficult conversations relaying very sad news will only bring your spirits down even further, and it will also take up far more time than you readily have available. Find a way of managing how to keep them up to date that isn't going to add to your pain.

This might be to ask one person to contact everyone on your behalf, or leave a new, updated voicemail message on your phone every day for people to listen to, or update your Facebook page once a day, or send everyone a daily group email or text.

Do not answer the phone or your mobile unless you feel up to it. That's why voicemail was invented.

Some people in life energise you and make you feel good, while others drain you of every last drop. Be discerning about who you spend time with, surround yourself with the people who do you the most good, right now it isn't the time to "carry passengers", particularly ones who fill you with negativity.

Maybe your child hasn't been given a diagnosis. Maybe you just have a nagging fear and sixth sense that things aren't right. It's very easy to feel that you're just wasting everybody's time and being a nuisance. You are not. Keep going, listen to your instinct and to your inner voices, and believe them. If I hadn't persisted, Toby would be dead.

CHAPTER 2
He said.... she said......

Shock affects people in very different ways, and what sometimes happens is that both parents deal with things in polar opposite ways. This can lead to all sorts of misunderstandings, upsets, rows and pained silences, just at the very time you need each other more than ever, and you child needs both parents to pull together and support each other.

There are as many ways of processing this sort of bad news as there are people, but there can also be a huge gender divide in the way shock is handled, too. It would be the stuff that highly-successful sitcoms are made of if it wasn't all so tragically damaging and hurtful. It can actually make each of you feel as if you're living with a stranger.

If you are part of a relationship where each of you deal with problems and handle emotions completely differently, you can both suddenly feel very isolated and alone within that relationship. Every couple is different, and just to show what can go wrong, please don't be offended, but I'm going to use the reactions of a couple who would each be at opposite extreme ends of our cultural gender stereotypes.

So we would have a mother who deals with emotions by expressing them outwardly, and who would need to talk the situation over and over and over again, before they can reach the point of getting through it all and reaching some form of acceptance. She would also feel a need to have her feelings validated by her partner and a whole circle of friends and family offering unlimited comfort, compassion and sympathy until she has virtually exhausted all her many confusing emotions.

The father, on the other hand, would have a tendency to be more task-orientated, looking for concrete solutions and fact-based ways forward. He would also display a tendency to want to deal with his emotions privately, needing lots of solitary time alone with his thoughts, but he would also have a deep-seated need to keep himself busy and occupied as well.

If both parents are rooted in these different models of behaviour, without any understanding of how their partner's reaction is equally valid and acceptable, it can lead to untold misery and stress with the relationship.

In these circumstances, it's very easy for the mother to feel her partner has transformed himself into an insensitive robot, while the father is equally concerned by the way his partner has evolved into an emotional blob.

She will be looking at him and misinterpreting his lack of outward emotion as a sign that he is uncaring, aloof and lacking humanity or decency. So in an effort to drive home to him just how serious this whole situation really is, she may react by doubling her efforts to cry, sob, rant and wail in hopeless despair. She will think this will bring him to his senses, but in fact it will drive him away even further.

He, meanwhile, is looking at her totally appalled that, just when they need to be taking a logical, measured and practical approach, she has started falling apart and having some sort of emotional breakdown. So, in turn, he may react by doubling his efforts to be practical and logical, knowing full well that he can't possibly fall apart too and show any unmanly weakness like tears. He, too, will believe that this is going to help matters, but all she will see is a confirmation of how utterly uncaring he is.

You can see what can happen here, can't you? It can be the beginning of a huge crack in the relationship, made worse by stuffing that crack full of misunderstandings, resentments, hurt and despair. It's hardly surprising that there's a sky-high divorce rate among parents of disabled children, but that doesn't have to happen to you.

It's easier said than done, but trying to understand that we all have different ways of coping really does help, even if the differences are not as marked as the example above. If you can find a way to give each other the time and space and loving non-judgement to handle things the way that you each need to, even if that way does seems alien and strange to you, your relationship will become stronger and closer with a deeper level of mutual respect, love, and an ability to carry each other through the worst of times. You both may need help to get to this point, and many couples really benefit by talking together with someone else about these issues, maybe a counsellor who isn't emotionally involved with the family.

Many parents describe this period of time as being like a bereavement, a process of grieving the child you thought you had before you can accept the child you actually have.

For me personally, it was never like that at all. It was more like having to take on board that the child I already knew has extra burdens to carry, and coming to terms with this new knowledge of how much tougher their life will be. I clearly remember being quite confused when people would say to me things like "Oh my goodness, I am so sorry, you really don't deserve this", and thinking that this actually isn't about me, it's about how much Toby doesn't deserve it. He was so small and vulnerable and innocent, and he was the one suffering the pain, fear and distress every time the doctors were working on him so hard to save his life.

The range of emotions you are likely to experience will sometimes hit you like a brick, completely unexpectedly. They will also sometimes frighten you, because sometimes these emotions can often be very negative, unpleasant ones, feelings that start making you think you are a horrible person.

Go with your feelings, accept them, and don't beat yourself up over them. Remember I was the one who ran away the moment I was told about Toby. Some parents struggle with moments when they actually wonder if it would be better if their child died, and then have to cope with feelings of intense guilt and betrayal for allowing those unthinkable issues to fleetingly pass through their thoughts.

I also hate to admit this, but for years I could not bring myself to look at any child born after Toby who was healthy. It doesn't make me feel like a very nice person at all, but those feelings were so real, so intense and I certainly never invited them in. It was probably Adam coming along three years later and developing into a sunny, happy and delightful little boy that finally banished those feelings completely.

Some people handle these intense and very painful feelings in ways that aren't helpful to themselves or those around them. Some use alcohol to numb their pain, and can become angry, remote, withdrawn or even violent, taking the problems of a family already under stress to a new level entirely. Others just bottle all their feelings up completely and try to carry on as if nothing has changed. One day that bottle may explode, causing untold distress and possibly damage.

These are times of extreme grief and sorrow, and it can be helpful to understand that there are identified stages of grief that people can go through while they are assimilating life-changing news, before they can reach a point where they can absorb it properly, accept it and begin to move on. However, not everyone reacts in the same way, and these stages are by no means universal, clearly recognisable or compulsory. Others may dip into one or two of these stages, or do them in an entirely different order, or get stuck in one stage for what seems like ages. It doesn't matter, we're all individuals, we all feel and experience things differently, so just accept things and go with the flow.

Don't forget that, to a greater or lesser extent, there may be a whole circle of people close to you who are also struggling to assimilate the news that your child has a disability. It can be very tough for close friends and family as well.

This is something else that's helpful to remember. There are many different stages of grief, and there also may be many people who are close to you and also very upset by this sad news. At any given time, everyone may be at a completely different stage of their grief, and also handling it in many different ways. This can make it hard to relate to people who actually care very deeply, but may be temporarily coping with such different feelings that it feels hard to find common ground.

Broadly speaking, these are the stages of grief that you may, or may not, go through.

Denial

This is a very common feeling, along the lines of "This can't be happening, and it certainly can't be happening to me and my family". This is a very common step along the process, and it makes sense, because it's easier to pretend it isn't real than to accept everything this new reality really means. Sometimes it may be members of the wider family or close friends who are expressing these feelings, simply because they just don't want it to be true.

Anger

After Toby, I got stuck in this one for a very long time. I held it together and never actually thumped anyone, but I was often very snappy and quick to lose my temper at the people who love me most. Losing my temper felt like a huge release, and luckily I have a lovely, understanding and very caring family, but it was never fair on any of them. Looking back, I now realise that I was terrified of crying, because I always felt that if I gave in to the tears they would never, ever stop. Sometimes getting cross with other adult members of my family felt much safer, and, even though I knew it was unfair, it meant that those tears I was feeling, prickling at the back of my eyes, were stopped dead in their tracks.

Guilt

I'm afraid this goes with the territory of parenthood, but particularly if your child is seriously ill or has disabilities. Maybe you think it was all your fault. Maybe you remember that one moment during pregnancy when you didn't quite remember to look after yourself properly for your baby's sake. You can start questioning the safety of cleaning products you may have used, the fumes you may have inhaled in traffic, that little lump of cheese from the back of the fridge that you weren't too sure of but you simply couldn't resist.... don't even start going there!! None of us are saints, and you simply wouldn't be human if you managed a whole nine months of tickety boo perfection. This was not your fault in any way, shape or form.

Most people have no prior experience of children like ours, and may even have had some negative prejudices and misconceptions about various disability issues until now. Overcoming the perceptions you may already have, and to then try to apply new ones to your child can have you in a tailspin of guilt and inner turmoil. Remember, none of us asked for this, but you will love your child always and beyond measure for who they are, even if you can't see right now how that will ever happen.

Maybe you feel that you aren't doing enough to help your child with meeting developmental milestones, or loving your child enough, or proving to the world and yourself that you are a good parent. Maybe you're harbouring negative thoughts towards your child and feel resentful or angry or hateful towards them. Whatever it is, don't beat yourself up. There are very few parents who haven't guilt-tripped themselves over something or another, and when disability is added to the mix, guilt is very normal. Disability and serious illness happen, usually at random, and it's so unfair that we all have moments of intense self-blame, but you'll sometimes feel it even though deep down you know there was nothing you could really have done to prevent it. I like to think that these guilt-ridden moments motivated me to love my three children that little bit more, but I loved them all so much anyway I'm not sure if it was even possible.

Grief

This floods in once you begin to accept things. It feels overwhelmingly painful, and you have times when you really don't feel you will ever be happy again. It will pass. Just keep saying that phrase over and over again, because it will pass, I promise.

Relief

Like all the stages, this can take many forms. Maybe you are so relieved that your niggling doubts and worries have been confirmed, your child's difficulties have been acknowledged and perhaps even named, and now you child will begin to get the help and understanding they deserve. Maybe you are relieved because the grief and anger are beginning to lift, and you feel like there may be happy times ahead to look forward to. Maybe there's relief because you can see that things could be much worse for your child, and are beginning to see things from a slightly more positive perspective. As you get used to the news, your feelings can shift and things don't seem as bleak and as hopeless as they did when the news was recent and raw. Sometimes for me it was just catching a glimpse of Toby's infectious grin, and being so pleased that in the midst of all the pain and sadness, he could still be happy.

Acceptance

No, I'm not joking, you will get there. There will come a time when you will be bursting with pride and joy and love like you've never felt before for your child, and with a bond that is stronger than steel.

The "But"

There is always a "But". Once you've gone through all these stages and you think you're back on an even keel and coping well with everything, there will be times when something happens and you're overwhelmed by all these negative, difficult and painful feelings all over again. It might be when a friend is thrilled that their child is walking and you know your child never will. It might be seeing all the local children going off to school happily, and you know your child will be going to another school miles away, wearing a different school uniform, just because of their condition. It may be years later, when you send another of your children off to University and you are thrilled for them, but at the same time you find yourself flooded with an all-pervading sadness for the child of yours who will never be going down that same exciting path. Sometimes it's the tactless remark that somebody makes, or hearing about another family going on a type of holiday that your family could never manage. It comes in all shapes and sizes, but that sadness often lurks in the shadows waiting to jump out at you and say "Boo!" when you're off-guard and least expecting it.

And now.... For some good news!

It gets easier over time, and you'll become much more resilient and able to bounce back again quickly, but you'll never completely be free of occasional moments of wistful sadness and "what if" yearnings. I find sharing them with close friends sometimes helps, and we often end up laughing about them to take the sting out of the hurt, and the world seems good and the horizon rosy all over again, once you find a way to laugh at anything.

TIPS, TRICKS AND STRATEGIES

Accept that everyone has their own way of dealing with life-changing events, and you and your partner may do things very differently.

Find time for each other, keep communicating as lovingly as you possibly can, and remember your partner, your other children, your wider family and the people who really care about you are hurting too. Their actions and words may not feel supportive at the moment, sometimes it can feel that it's a million miles away from being supportive, but they are doing their very best to come to terms with this news, and there is almost certainly no deliberate intention to hurt you.

Accept that you will feel overwhelmed by all sorts of feelings, some of which may be very difficult to cope with, and some of which may seem to make no sense whatsoever. Just accept them, accept that this is going to be a difficult period of adjustment, and just let the feelings flow.

Cry buckets if you need to. Distance yourself if you need to. Do whatever feels right at the moment.

Remember it will pass. Things will get easier, you will come to terms with things and there will be plenty of good times ahead.

Tell family and close friends as soon as you can. It can be hard to break the news, but they can't help and support you unless they understand.

Don't expect everyone to understand how you are feeling all the time. They don't have a crystal ball or second sight. Tell them if you can, or explain at times of less intense feelings, how sometimes feelings just overwhelm you and they need to step back, or step forward, or cope with your uncontrollable anger for a while. Reassure them that you love them, and ask them to bear with you.

Look after yourself, and look out for your partner too. If either one of you is struggling too hard and is beginning to not cope well at all, please seek help. In extreme circumstances, one partner may overflow with anger or extreme emotion to the point where you or the children may be at risk. This is not a situation you can cope with alone. Safety and getting help become the only priorities. If you are concerned things may be heading in this direction, talk it over with someone, preferably your GP, but let friends and family know too. If your family reaches a crisis point where you may be in danger, call 999 immediately.

Remember your other children. No matter how young, they will know that something upsetting is happening, and they need lots of extra love, affection, reassurance and time. Sometimes children have a tendency to blame themselves if they don't know what's going on and why. Tell them as much as you can in a positive and age-appropriate way. If you aren't strong enough to do this yourself, ask a grandparent or other trusted adult to talk to them and give them space to ask plenty of questions.

It will pass. You will feel better. Yes I know I've just said that already, but you may need to hear it more than once to start believing it.

Don't be afraid to ask for help. Practical help, emotional help, whatever help you think might help.

Don't allow your imagination to run too far into the future, because that will scare the living daylights out of you. Deal with the now, in ten minute chunks of time at a time if that will help. The future will take care of itself, and things will probably all work out much better than you could ever imagine right now.

Last of all, with the best will and the biggest effort in the world, sometimes a relationship will never recover from something as enormous as this. Make sure you've done what you can and that you've given it sufficient time, but you may have to both accept that it's over. If it's come to this point, the sooner you can make that decision and each move on separately with your lives, the easier it will be and the more amicable you will feel towards each other, even if it's an incredibly painful and difficult decision to reach. Dragging it on when your relationship has reached its "sell-by" date does nothing but make you both thoroughly miserable, and therefore with less energy or resources to support your child. I know this and so does my ex-husband. We stubbornly held on for about 10 more long years after it was clear to everyone, ourselves included, that we had passed the point of no return. Somehow, despite the hurts and emotional injuries we both sustained in that decade of unhappiness, Chris and I are still on good terms, acknowledging we are both significantly happier now we have parted.

CHAPTER 3
The Advancing Army of Professionals

There's no easy way to say this, but life as you know it will never be the same again. Your child's condition will bring you into contact with untold numbers of people you never expected to meet. Over the next few years, but sometimes starting immediately, there will be dozens of new people in your life from various organisations and with varying degrees of expertise and experience. Broadly speaking, they come from three main areas of the statutory services; Health, Education and Social Care, although there may also be people from other organisations such as charities. Parents of children with disabilities have a generic term for all these people; we call them "Professionals". It's something of a misnomer because, at times, a very small proportion of these individuals are anything but professional, unfortunately.

Sometimes it will seem that these professionals are all queuing around the block to spend time with you, either in your own living room or elsewhere, and there will be times when you feel that you may as well remove the whole of the front wall of your house and let everybody in to have a good look around, because it can quickly feel as if you are living in a goldfish bowl.

You'll meet people who will make you want to weep with gratitude for their kindness, insight, and the way they are happy to go that extra mile to help your child. There will be others you will cheerfully want to strangle. Some will raise your spirits and make you feel like the world is a wonderful place; others will add completely avoidable stress, anxiety and despair to your household, usually on the very days which weren't going particularly well in the first place.

You quickly learn to work out which of them "get it" and which of them don't, and then you learn a harder lesson; it's almost impossible to get the ones who just don't "get it" off your case. You often have to put up with them for years, until your child's care is moved to another completely different team in Adult Services.

It can feel like an invading army, and although they really aren't the enemy, the way your privacy gets trampled all over makes them feel like an invading force. Friendly fire is also a fairly common occurrence and it can feel as if they are all joining forces just to ruin your day. At first, it just all seems overwhelmingly intrusive at times, but not only do you get used to it, you also eventually learn how to make these meetings and appointments work out in the best possible way to the benefit of your child.

In fairness to these professionals, most of them are really lovely, kind people with their hearts in the right places. One of the benefits of having children like mine is that I have been privileged to meet some inspiring, dedicated and totally committed people, wonderful individuals who will do whatever it takes to achieve the very best outcomes for my family. Some of them you start to consider as friends, particularly if, as in my case when Toby was very small, I was isolated at home, and most of the adults I saw were these very professionals. However, they have to keep a professional distance, and although you may bond with them very well and be able to share both the laughs and the tears of your predicament, they are never able to completely step across that divide to become friends. The nature of your relationships with these people has to be one-sided; they will know far more about you and your life than they can ever share with you about theirs. There will always therefore be a marked, if subtle, difference; there will always be an inequality of status in the relationship.

Most professionals are far too thoughtful and empathetic to deliberately highlight this inequality, but it's there, hanging tangibly in the air, like an elephant in the room, and I always keenly felt it, that I am of less importance and value than the professional. When you have whole teams, or huge armies as it sometimes felt, of professionals coming in to help, or to suggest, or to add another task to Toby's already overloaded care-plan, I couldn't help but start to lose my self-esteem, self-confidence and sense of worth. I was always apologising and always thanking, both rituals further continually underlining to me my own inferiority.

It's very easy to get crushed by the enormity of the system supposedly there to support the children, and despite the very best efforts of the very best professionals, it's very hard to maintain a sense of dignity and status.

It's not the fault of the individual professional, it's the relentlessness of the system, the way services never quite join up and there is never enough money to really be able to make a difference, and the way my privacy, my autonomy as a mother, and my whole life was subsumed by their constant presence. That's not to say I don't have hugely fond memories of most of those from Toby's early days, but this wasn't the way I would have chosen to bring my children up, and the frequency of the intrusiveness was hard to cope with. When they suggested something new to try, it often felt more like an imperative order than simply advice, and each time it felt that I was expected to rush around even faster, never quite catching my tail, and losing just that little bit more of what very limited control I had over our family's life.

There are so many people who have been involved with my family over the years, hundreds if not thousands of nurses, doctors, care assistants, school staff, social care personnel, and it is to their credit that the overwhelming majority have been a total pleasure to deal with.

People being people, though, particularly when you are dealing with such a large number, there have been a handful that have made our lives very difficult indeed. Altogether, only about 7 or 8 professionals in total over all those years, but it only takes one who you feel is working against you to cause untold harm to the equilibrium of the multi-disciplinary team as a whole. These few let all the others down, and the upset they cause can be proportionately much greater than their tiny numbers merit.

We've had certain professionals who have appeared to have taken a personal dislike towards our family. It's very difficult when this happens, particularly when they talk privately and share their personal views with other professionals.

There have been times when I sensed a very real whispering campaign going on behind the scenes, an almost imperceptible cooling of the warmth towards me previously extended by other professionals, and I have known that anything I try to say or do to counter this change in attitude will be futile. These professionals can also tarnish a family's reputation by writing comments on reports and other documents. Once written, it's almost impossible to get such comments retracted or removed. The power and the credibility is stacked in their favour.

Professionals are encouraged to "share information", and unfortunately, there are simply not enough checks and balances within the current system to ensure that the information they are sharing is correct. Sometimes it is incorrect, incomplete, conjecture, opinion, or in a very tiny number of instances, downright damaging. A lot of this "information" is communicated "off the record", so there is nothing parents in my situation can do to be sure of what might have been said, but sometimes you know with certainty that things have been said which are both unfair and untrue.

The way the system works makes it very difficult for other professionals to come to your aid at these times, the times you need support the most. There is an unspoken closing of ranks and an expectation to show loyalty towards the other professionals. Within the public sector working culture, whistle-blowers have a really tough time of it, and many careers have been ruined because decent professionals have spoken out. So when the chips are down, they have no choice but to cover for each other, even if that means that you and your family are left out in the cold.

Frustrating, difficult, infuriating and unjust as it is, there is very little you can do about it. I just make sure that I am doing all I can to keep in regular contact with all the other professionals, and being as pleasant and friendly as I can possibly be. Actions speak louder than words – I always hope that they will realise that I'm a decent person with a lot of integrity, and eventually I have ridden out the storm each time. But it can take one heck of a long time.

Health

You may see also dozens of doctors over the next few years. Toby had 14 different Consultants for several years, each wanting to see him in clinic regularly, either at 3-monthly or 6-monthly intervals. That meant we often had 42 important hospital appointments every year, or nearly one every week. Factor in Physiotherapists, Speech and Language Therapists, Dieticians, Community Nurses and Orthotic Practitioners etc, and you begin to get a picture of how exhausting the whole thing can become. Later on, Dysphagia Nurses, Incontinence Nurses and Specialist Behaviour Therapists were also added to our mix. Over and over again, you'll find yourself explaining the same things to different people, or different things to the same people. A lot of these meetings all run into one long mess of a memory now.

Just because Toby had disabilities, it didn't make him immune to the normal illnesses and accidents of childhood, so on top of that there were also plenty of unscheduled trips to our GP and our Accident and Emergency Department as well. Altogether, it was a rare week when we didn't have at least two medical appointments in a single week, and to have three or four in a week was not uncommon. The appointment scheduling is always done for the professionals' convenience, never for yours, so we have had some exhausting weeks with eleven appointments squeezed in between Monday and Friday. Over time, I did learn to be quite assertive in getting appointments changed to be more manageable, but sometimes it's just not possible; there can be months longer to wait to see a particular paediatric specialist if you want to change an appointment to a more convenient time-slot.

Social Care

For many parents, being referred to Social Services is the stuff of nightmares. Not everyone is aware that within every local authority there is a Social Work Team specifically in place to support families with disabled children, normally aptly named something like "The Children with Disabilities Social Work Team".

When I was first told that a Social Worker would be coming to see me at home, I was scared stiff, paranoid and defensive. I assumed they must be on their way because somebody thought I wasn't good enough as a mother, and that they were going to take Francesca and Toby away there and then. I wondered if I ought to barricade us in the house or drive off into the yonder to somewhere we couldn't easily be found. Driving away with the massive amount of Toby's medical equipment was nigh on impossible, and we didn't have enough food in the house to stay barricaded for very long, so I decided to face the music and let the social worker in.

I'm so glad I did, because that was the first time I met the social worker who would be with us, on and off, for very many years, and fortunately she was definitely one of those who "got it". It always felt she was on our side, and she would help me move heaven and earth to get the very best for all my children. We were incredibly lucky to have a Social Worker who it felt was mostly singing from the same song-sheet, and it was lovely when, after a gap of several years, she was reallocated to our family when Toby was 14, and stayed with us until she handed over his care to the Adult Services Team on his 18th birthday.

However, just because we had a great social worker didn't mean we were totally pleased and delighted with each and every outcome from the Social Services department, far from it. There were plenty of skirmishes and scuffles along the way, as there always will be, I'm afraid.

Education

For kids like Toby, the education system can kick in when they are only a few months old, with a visiting "Portage Worker" coming to your house every week. They work with your child and you to help them do things and explore the world in ways that might come easily for most children, but are significantly harder for your child. Almost universally, families fall in love with their portage worker from the very beginning. Generally, they are full of information, warmth and encouragement, they can introduce you to other local families with similar struggles, and it feels like they are your very own cheerleading beacon of hope. Many parents find that it is their relationship with their portage worker that helps them gain a brighter perspective on everything and to really begin to believe that there is going to be light at the end of the tunnel.

It's often your portage worker who will gently ease you towards some big decisions that will need to be thought about and made when your child is still very tiny – decisions about different types of school options, and the whole Statementing or EHCP process, a process which will continue to be a dominant feature of families like ours all the way through our children's school-days, and legally defines exactly what extra help each child with disabilities must receive whilst at school. (Statementing and EHCP processes are explained more fully in Chapter 13).

Budgets

It also becomes very clear very quickly, that everything is much more about money and budgets than about what your child actually needs. Even more infuriating is when they know exactly what your child needs, but play games to protect their own budgets and try to pass the financial responsibility of a crucial service or piece of equipment onto a different department or organisation. Meanwhile, your child goes without while they play interdepartmental politics.

The ever-growing Admin-Mountain

Then there's the paperwork. Like you just wouldn't believe. Forms for this, applications for that, emails to send, phone-calls to make, it just never ever stops. Every single one of the endless non-stop meetings you have to attend on behalf of your child will have had minutes produced, and these are sent to you to check their accuracy. Sometimes, you will look at these minutes, and they are so far away from your own recollection of the meeting that you begin to wonder if you were actually at the same meeting that they purport to represent. So when you have finished with your own feelings of shock, seething anger and disbelief, you will then have to set about making notes to construct a letter to send back to challenge these minutes, and to request changes you feel would better describe what actually happened.

You begin to feel like you're drowning in administration. You want to stop it somehow but you can't. Even if you bricked up your letterbox to stop the avalanche of mail pouring through your front door, they can still catch you out with emails or phone-calls or even just turn up in person at your door to personally hand you yet more reams of paper.

You'll soon have boxes of stuff to read, stuff to write, stuff to fill out and then you'll have to make time to file it all. Never throw anything away. Sometimes I've had to find a precious piece of paper from six or seven years ago to prove my case and get my children the services or treatment they desperately need. It is a nightmare. My admin mountain once spread across seven large plastic boxes, and on one memorable occasion I pushed the sofa out three feet into the room to make space behind it to hide the wretched boxes.

It's bad enough the amount they generate for one child, but I've had three of them to use as an excuse to bombard me with more and more bits of paper to control and tame. My family has probably been single-handedly responsible for entire forests being destroyed, just to torment me with building that admin mountain ever higher and pushing me closer to the very edge of sanity.

When you tell people that you can't cope with this overload of paper, they look surprised and just can't grasp it. They assume you must be a bit late in paying an electricity bill or an unpaid parking fine, but this stuff is on a different level altogether.

Every time a health professional sees your child they send a letter to your GP, and a copy comes to you. Every letter has to be read because you would be amazed at how often they get their facts wrong. One very common example for us is that Toby has Pseudo Bulbar Palsy, but more often than not this is translated onto paper as Cerebal Palsy, a totally different condition which he does not have. If it goes unchecked, there is a risk that he could be given the wrong treatment one day, which could potentially endanger his health. Or the list of his drugs is transposed incorrectly or the dosages are wrongly copied down. Getting these things changed and corrected can then take several phone calls and letters, and you often get stuck in the middle as the go-between to both the Consultant concerned and your GP. Even when these issues are finally resolved, it's not over. You may then find yourself contacting everyone else who may or may not have received a copy of the original letter, trying to persuade them to destroy the original incorrect version. If you don't, no one else will, and it will be you who has to sort out the mess if the wrong letter is produced and the wrong treatment given several years down the line.

I carry a load of guilt that the paperwork mountain never nears the bottom, and there have been days I've cried like a baby when the postman has just delivered another batch of admin that has to be added to the mountain. I have often woken up in the middle of the night panicky and anxious because I know I've missed deadlines and missed out on funding or lost out on getting things ordered in time.

Then I get phone-calls from bossy receptionists and clerks chasing particular pieces of paper, saying really irritating things like "well, it will only take a couple of minutes to fill in". Yes I know that, but multiply that by 100 other forms and there simply isn't the time in the day to do it all.

If I was doing it all over again, I would digitalise a lot of the filing, but in the mid-nineties we didn't have the technology. I would scan every piece of paper that needed to be kept, and I would have a dedicated external hard drive to file them on, with cross references across different subject areas to make them really easy to find several years later when some ancient difficulty comes up from nowhere and bites you on the bum. You will always need to keep originals filed safely; I have numerous lever-arch ring binders for each of the children, with everything in individual transparent punched pockets and filed away in strict chronological order, with a page at the front of each ring-binder listing out every document contained within that particular file. Filing takes forever, and I tend to have major blitz filing days two or three times a year.

A little DLA/PIP idea

Filling out a Disability Living Allowance form, which will be replaced at some point with a Personal Independence Payment, has to be one of the most soul-destroying aspects of all the administration tasks put together. I now measure the boxes, and adjusting the font/typeface to fit, I type it all up as a Word document, print it out, and glue the printed piece of paper to the form itself. This works well for two reasons; firstly, you can write much more than you could by hand which is sometimes the only way to describe things well, and secondly, when DLA/PIP form time comes around again, sometimes only a year or two later, you'll have all the answers saved and so the subsequent forms are virtually written already.

Why is it soul-destroying? It's a 40-page form with most pages having blank boxes to write your own narrative explanations of how your child's disability impacts on this, that and the other aspects of their life. Every parent likes to "big-up" their child's qualities, characteristics and achievements, it's a natural part of parenting to want to sing their child's praises to the rooftops. Not on these forms, though. You have to painstakingly reveal in very negative terms everything that is different and harder for your child. You have to come face to face with everything you want to keep privately locked away, and it makes you feel very vulnerable, very sad and lost, and for me and for many of my friends in a similar situation, the whole application form is desperately depressing and brings right up to the surface all over again every single ounce of the pain you've ever felt for your child having their condition, and the fact that, as a parent, there is nothing you can do to make things better.

The ever-growing list of therapeutic interventions

When you see as many therapists as we did, they each add on little bits and pieces to the burden of your day. I was already preparing and administering tube feeds to Toby every two hours throughout the day and night, so I was surviving on next to no sleep. Then I had to factor in chest physiotherapy 4 times a day too, being careful to avoid times when he had just been fed in case it made him vomit. Then he was prescribed nebulisers, using a machine that delivered a fine mist of a drug through a mask covering his mouth and nose, 6 doses of one drug, four of another, plus two of a third drug in a 24 hour period. Sometimes they could be given together but that would take ages, sometimes over half an hour, particularly because I had to dilute it with saline to make it a much larger volume which seemed to take forever. Two of these drugs had to be always given 20 minutes before each chest physio session. Chest physio sessions would take 15 minutes, nebulisers nearly 20 minutes, and tube feeds, including preparing them and staying with him for 15 minutes after he had finished in case he vomited, took another 40 minutes.

Then he had to be strapped into a standing frame for two sessions of half an hour a day. We had to do our portage homework every day. We had an oxygen saturation monitor that Toby wore on his foot at night, and it would alarm if the oxygen levels in his blood plummeted, which was the only way I would be alerted to the fact that he was having difficulty breathing. If I needed to leave the room to go to the loo, or to put washing away, or to cook, I had to put this "Sats Monitor" on him every time. He was also on a whole stack of drugs, 18 in all, which had to be mixed in water and then put into syringes and into his feeding-tube with another syringe of water to flush it through.

I never stopped. I never drew breath. It was like being on a speeding hamster wheel with physics, maths, chemistry and biology thrown in for good measure.

Always back-footed

The house was never tidy or clean or presentable. The professionals would arrive, all refreshed after a relaxing weekend and decent sleep every night, looking suited and booted and manicured and with perfectly applied make-up. I looked like the madwoman from hell, with a filthy house and hair that hadn't seen a comb for days on end. I was always back-footed.

Other women, I'm sure, will know exactly what I mean when I talk about that "eye thing" a certain type of woman does to you, an almost imperceptible looking you up and down, taking in every single one of your imperfections, and letting their judgemental eye linger just that nanosecond too long so that you know full well you've been tested and you've failed. Just because that type of woman may also have a professional qualification which automatically confers a higher status than yours, it doesn't mean that they won't do it all the same, as if they just really want to drive home to you the fact of your inferiority.

It got to the point where I began to feel that in every encounter with a professional I was being judged and patronised and being set up to fail again and again and again.

Then there is the jargon. When you're new to it, it might as well be a foreign language, and this jargon often gets used in meetings by those in the know, conveniently excluding those of us in the don't-know. When you feel excluded from the conversation, you lose your voice and you can't be part of the decision-making process either. In time I learnt the jargon, and I also developed enough confidence to question the phrases I didn't understand, but in those early years, it felt that this private language of theirs was sometimes being used as a tool to marginalise and silence me very effectively indeed.

Maintaining your dignity

In the middle of all of this there are some very useful things to remember.

One little trick I used was to play a particular mantra silently in my head over and over again, which I found useful to help me feel a little bit more empowered during this never-ending succession of meetings. It went like this:-

"They are the public servants, and my family are the public, so their job is to serve us, not the other way around."

In practical terms it didn't make any difference, probably, but just made me feel a bit better and that tiny little bit more assertive when I felt they were running their eyes a tad too judgementally over the clutter of the house or the fact that I often looked like a particularly unkempt Old Mother Hubbard who lived in a very shabby shoe.

Secondly, remember that manners are of the utmost importance. Try never to show your anger, no matter how worked up you feel inside. The minute you do, they've won. It shouldn't feel like a battle but it often does. You are going to have to find a way of working with these people for many years to come, and you can't afford to alienate any of them. I've learnt to use sweet reason and charm as a powerful ally over the years.

That said, there may be times when you are very angry about the way something is being done or not being done for your child. When I say never show your anger, what I really mean is that you get nowhere by table thumping, throwing your weight around and trying to threaten or intimidate them. However, if you are angry, it helps if you can learn how to express that anger in a measured, rational way. Basically, if you can practice stepping back and talking about your anger calmly in words, rather than showing your anger in actions, that's a great skill to develop and it is actually much more effective. Practise if necessary, either in front of a mirror, or with friends or family until you can confidently voice your anger calmly.

I am certainly not advocating bottling up your emotions completely and pretending everything is fine and dandy if it quite clearly isn't.

Thirdly, if you feel it will help, send an email within 24 hours with the most important points you made in the meeting. If you put your input in writing, they are much less likely to conveniently forget to record these points in the subsequent minutes of the meeting.

Fourthly, if it's going to be one of the many formal meetings about your child, always take someone with you into these meetings. If possible, somebody dressed very smartly, and have them bring a formal notebook and pen. Their job is to stay very quiet and take copious notes, or at least look as if they're taking copious notes. Doing this just very slightly back-foots the professionals, which can help to redress the balance of power a tiny bit back into your favour.

Lastly for now, never forget that each of the professionals you meet has made an active choice to work in this field, a choice that you never had the luxury of making. They work 8 hours a day and only 5 days a week. You never stop being a parent. They are paid good salaries with a pension scheme and other benefits, you are doing all of this for free. All in all, you are at that meeting and putting up with this whole new level of bureaucracy simply because you love your child and want the very best for them, whereas they are there because they have been told to turn up. So don't let them make you feel bad about yourself in any way, or put you down, or guilt-trip or back-foot you however hard they try. The moral high-ground is entirely yours.

TIPS, TRICKS AND STRATEGIES

Go into every meeting or appointment well prepared, with an idea of what you want to get out of it for your child.

Don't be afraid to say "No, I can barely cope with what I'm being expected to do already, I can't take on anymore."

Don't try and give the impression that you're a Super-parent. If they think you can cope they will let you struggle on and they won't ever offer any extra help.

If you feel pressured during the meeting, mentally step back, take a deep breath, maybe a sip of water to buy you some time to gather your thoughts, and then remember that this is about your child, and that you are their best advocate. You can do this.

Some parents I know take a framed photo of their child into every meeting and put it in the middle of the room where everyone can see it. Then they remind all those present that this is about the child and they would be very grateful if everyone could try and remember that. It is a great trick for taking control and placing your child in the centre of any discussions. It gently reminds the professionals around the table that the purpose of this meeting is supposed to be about your child, not about budgets, funding, hidden agendas, interdepartmental politics or any of the other nonsenses that often get played out around the table instead.

I've often done a similar thing; before the meeting, I show a recent, particularly funny or adorable photo of my child on my phone to all the professionals. It's more subtle, but you are still gently reminding them of the reason why this meeting has been called.

Try and step back and find a way not to take it all too seriously. If you can, there may even be aspects with a funny side to them. This is your new world, you can't afford to feel intense stress each and every time, and if you find a way to put it into a more manageable perspective, you'll find you can put your points across much more eloquently, and you will get a better outcome for your child time and again.

Try and learn the jargon and use it in these meetings. It helps you feel more of an equal among these people.

Don't take responsibility for everything. Bat some questions back to them and put them on the spot. Don't be a willing doormat-scapegoat for them, it's always so easy to overload the parents with all the therapies and treatments in the world, and it's also very easy for the parents to be blamed for everything. Keep your wits about you, and don't let it happen.

Try not to say things in the heat of the moment, and aim never to close any doors or to bite your own nose off to spite your face, but if you accidentally do, don't worry too much. Every time you get something wrong, you'll learn something valuable and be better placed to be able to cope with things at the next meeting.

You're new to this, they aren't. You're on a long, slow learning curve with none of the years of training, support and guidance they receive as an integral part of the job. You won't get it right every time, and certainly not in the beginning. As time goes on, you'll become better and better at it. After every meeting have a think and work out what went well and what didn't, and see if there are any patterns emerging. It might help you to keep notes of how you felt you handled each meeting, looking at what went wrong and what could have gone better, and were there any moments when you shot yourself in the foot. You can then build on this information for next time.

If professionals start using acronyms or jargon, interrupt, put them on the spot, and as nicely as possible, ask them to explain what they mean. They all do it, but they aren't supposed to, because it's now accepted that this isn't helpful for laypeople such as parents to properly take part in discussions. The more we point it out, the quicker we will help shift the culture so that it will soon become completely unacceptable.

Start cultivating the professionals you trust, and there will be some. Before any meeting, ring them up or pop in to see them and seek their advice, explain in the briefest possible terms any of your concerns and get them on side. Sometimes it's these people that end up fighting our corner for us without us having to do very much at all.

Always be early, and be willing to join in the small-talk before and after a meeting. Find common ground and find a way to laugh with them – making friends with them will pay dividends over and over again.

Sometimes it may be suggested that large meetings take place in your house. It's fine if it's just one or two people, but I hosted larger meetings at home several times and I would strongly advise against it. Firstly, you'll have the stress of making sure the house is clean and tidy before they arrive. Then you'll be the one running about making gallons of tea and coffee while they are making small talk, or even worse, continuing the meeting about your child while you're making their drinks. Then after the meeting, even though everyone has left, it can feel very difficult. The meeting atmosphere can linger for hours, you can still see and hear all the difficult moments much more vividly than you would if the meeting had happened elsewhere, and your house just doesn't feel like your home straight away.

CHAPTER 4
When the Dust Starts to Settle

There comes a time, beyond the shock and disbelief, when real life will kick in, and you have to find a way of picking up all the pieces and putting them back together again, but perhaps in a different order. This stage is unique to everyone and everybody's situation. It felt entirely different for me on each of the three occasions I had to handle this process, with the impact lesser or greater depending on a range of factors. So I'm going to base this chapter on the processes I had to cope with when Toby was very little. The changes his condition imposed on every aspect of my existence felt so raw and totally unmanageable. Hopefully your experience won't have been quite so difficult, but there will still be plenty of commonalities and emotions that you recognise in your own situation.

You have to face the fact that your child will never be quite the same as most other children. Please try and leave it there for the moment. Don't try and imagine how their life will be in years to come or you will, quite simply, go completely stark-raving, loopy-loo bonkers. You may end up doing what I used to do, getting really worked up over certain aspects of Toby's future, things that mostly never actually happened, or if they did, it all worked out absolutely fine.

Live in the Now

In those early days I broke my own heart a thousand times over by imagining a ten year old Toby being sad, lonely and friendless, with no self-worth or capacity for enjoyment whatsoever, and being ignored in the street because he would have lost his "aaah factor", the little boy cuteness that I felt made disability somehow more socially acceptable.

Well what a complete waste of tears and upset that one turned out to be! Toby is 19 now; you can't push his wheelchair down our High Street without about a dozen people stopping to chat to him or wave. If people do tune him out and ignore him (yes, of course it sometimes happens) he is hilarious. He will go to extreme lengths to catch their attention, normally by making really exaggerated vocal noises, you know the type of noise; the guttural shouts and squeals that only non-verbal learning disabled people like Toby can do really well. When they momentarily look across at him in an embarrassed "please don't let this be happening" sort of way, quick as a flash Toby will blow them a flamboyant kiss. The reactions he gets fall into two very distinct categories, either he'll win them over, and he'll get a huge smile break out across their face, or he won't, and they turn away and hurry off. Either way, you can just tell that Toby is highly amused - he may have the cognitive equivalent attainment of a neuro-typical two-year-old, but in some respects he operates at pure genius level.

Even better, somehow Toby has managed to retain his "aah factor" cuteness, too. His outrageous charm somehow just draws people in to him, makes them fall in love with him, and then manages to bring out the absolute best in most of them. So, in many respects, his quality of life is excellent. He just loves life and he finds all sorts of ways to milk the fun out of every moment. He is also a bit of a maverick anarchist on the quiet.

Don't try and think what life will be like too far ahead, because you will just cause yourself all sorts of grief and upset. Take things a day at a time; the future can wait.

In those early days, when sometimes getting through the whole day just seemed insurmountable, I became very successful at tackling life a bit at a time, never looking too far ahead. Sometimes I stumbled through for weeks on end tackling life in 10 minute chunks. When things are really tough, and you just don't know how you will get through until bedtime without losing the plot and collapsing in tears, just finding a way to get through the next ten minutes is always doable, then you can look to the next ten minutes and cope with getting through them too.

Feeling overwhelmed

In these early days, making adjustments and accepting change is very hard, and may take quite some time, even though the rawness and hurt of the initial bewilderment may be subsiding. There will be moments, or whole days or weeks, when you feel overwhelmed with difficult feelings such as anxiety, worry, sadness and feeling exhausted all the time. You may be blinking tears back a lot of the time or bursting into spontaneous floods of tears at the most inappropriate moments. You may find it difficult to be interested in anything whatsoever, things can feel very unimportant and shallow and superficial compared to the realities of your child's problems. You may experience physical symptoms such as headaches, stomach aches or feel that your heart is racing fast and thumping hard. You may lose your appetite entirely or comfort-eat like crazy. You might lie awake for hours every night consumed with all sorts of awful thoughts and feelings. Some people may withdraw and find it difficult to communicate with others, even very close friends and family, some may be overwhelmed with anger, and driven to take it out on everyone or become destructive.

Sometimes you may have very negative thoughts about your child or other children too. These can be very frightening, and they can also make you feel like you are a terrible person. You are not. It's all part of the "coming to terms" process. Due to no fault of your child or yourself, the whole landscape and fabric of your world has shifted irrevocably. Many parents, completely understandably, have moments of intense resentment, apportioning blame and real antipathy towards their child for being the catalyst of such a huge shift. Then they beat themselves up and experience profound guilt and self-hatred for being capable of such feelings. The feelings will pass, your boundless love and protective, compassionate instincts will overtake you again, and things will be OK.

Many parents are completely taken-aback by how they can become engulfed by their emotions, and when it feels that you are beginning to drown in one negative emotion after another, coming at you thick and fast with little time to catch your breath between each new one, it can be very frightening. Some parents worry that they are losing control, or that, in the grip of a really powerful emotion they may not be able to stop themselves from doing something that they will spend the rest of their life regretting.

Don't worry, most of us have an inner voice that will step in to protect you from potential actions, and cases like this are thankfully rare. However, if this type of thought is affecting you, try and turn it around and use those fears in a positive way. Work out what steps you can take if you feel yourself reaching a point where the emotions might just boil over, and formulate a plan in your head. I had trigger points where, if I felt myself reaching, I knew to stop still, acknowledge the emotion, take several deep breaths, walk away from the children, ring someone to ask them to come over, or even if they couldn't, just hearing a friendly voice on the end of the phone helped hugely. Sometimes, I just needed to distance myself from the children, go out into the garden, lean against a wall, and after a couple of minutes the blackness would pass and I'd be able to cope all over again.

I think people would be surprised to discover that there are probably a huge number of parents like us who harbour a "there but for the grace of God" moment, a memory when they were only a whisker away from doing, in a terrible, momentary state of turmoil, something simply awful. If parents of children who are developing normally sometimes feel like that, these feelings can be magnified out of all proportion for parents of children like ours. Sometimes the stress just takes over, the depths of despair are so profound, and the sense of helplessness so painful that, just for a nano-second, it pulls us into a dark place of completely losing the plot.

These feelings are part of the whole processing period, and if they persist there is all sorts of help that can be accessed through either your GP or your local social services, and no one will judge you for acknowledging these feelings and being sufficiently in control not to act upon them, but to ask for help instead.

There are trained professionals who can speed up the "coming to terms with" period and also help you examine what extra resources you need to cope with your new situation. Social Services can arrange for carers to come into your house to give you a break, or to help with your other children or with other chores, or sometimes even to offer overnight respite for your child so that you can step back and relax and share some of this new overwhelming responsibility with others.

However, just because there is help out there, it doesn't mean you'll easily be able to access it, because the professionals will guard their budgets as if their lives depended on it. If you really need help, be persistent.

Asking for help is a strength, not a weakness

It's difficult to convey just how lonely, frightened, lost and overloaded I felt during those early years, and I wish I'd had the ability to step back, take stock, and to ask for the right sort of help very early on. For years I was running on empty. Toby's care was so full-on. Gastrostomy feeding, holding a syringe filled with milk high in the air and letting it drip slowly through directly into his stomach, while watching all the time for the first signs of vomiting, which happened several times a day.

When Toby vomitted, it was just as likely to be aspirated directly into his lungs as it was to come out of his mouth. Sometimes it was projectile vomiting which would go everywhere, but every time he vomitted, I knew that some of it would have slipped down his airway. Every vomit was a medical emergency, I'd have to drop the syringe, pull him out of his little chair, lie him on his side on the floor in the recovery position whilst gently thumping his back, hoping against hope that he would find the strength to cough all the vomit up from his lungs so that we wouldn't be facing yet another very serious chest infection within the next 48 hours. Throughout all the rising panic I would be feeling, I also had to keep Francesca safe. She was still not quite 2 years old and going through the bumps and bruises stage of toddlerhood. I would give her little jobs to do, her favourite one became holding Toby's hand and singing songs to him.

Those moments weren't even the worst of it. Not even the constant clearing up of sick on the carpet, all over the sofa and the walls and our clothing. Not even the moments when Toby stopped breathing and despite all the CPR I was taught, time would hang in the air for what seemed like a lifetime while he went blue and I was sure this time we were losing him. Or the total and utter loss of privacy or freedom or being able to go out and get the basics, like milk and bread, in the house. Or the night after night of sitting up alone watching and waiting until the next feed, or nebuliser, or chest physio or drugs had to be administered, and hoping against hope that he would stay asleep and breathing while I waited. It was the complete and utter imprisonment to time and space and hopelessness, because I always knew that, at any moment, things would deteriorate with Toby to such a degree that I'd be calling 999 for an ambulance to take us, yet again, to hospital for goodness knows how many weeks at a time.

Over his first 5 years, he was blue-lighted to hospital 38 times, more often than not in the middle of the night. I would have to wait until the ambulance arrived and the paramedics could stay with Toby while I knocked on neighbours' doors with a sleeping Francesca in my arms asking if they could take her for me....again. They were wonderful. My neighbours were like family, they were an integral part of my lifeline.

No, the worst of all of it was being admitted to hospital, knowing that I had failed to keep Toby safe and well, and knowing that I would again lose control of the decisions about his care. It was slowly dawning on me that when you have a SWAN child, the only child in the world with his condition, I was becoming his expert, I was intuitively aware of when he was struggling and what might resolve it. Toby, like many SWAN children, never presented his symptoms in a textbook way and he simply baffled the doctors. I could sense what was around the corner and how ill he was about to become, and what they could do to prevent him crashing. They needed to see him crash first, then scratch their heads and decide which of the many conventional options might be best.

Time after time we nearly lost him; and it was made crystal clear all the way through that this child wasn't for this planet for very long; he was never expected to survive beyond a year or two, then definitely not beyond his fifth birthday, then not to dare hope that he'd ever reach his teenage years.

The worst times, without a doubt were spent night after night, week after week, sometimes month after month on a camp-bed on the floor next to his cot in a tiny side room, isolated, alone and frightened.

I honestly thought I wasn't doing enough to keep Toby well and out of hospital, and I was too proud to admit to even myself that I wasn't able to cope, and that I was close to breaking point. So I could never have said it to them.

One thing I know now that I didn't know then was that professionals, be they medical, social care or education staff, have a hidden agenda to minimise how bad things are and how tough life really is for us.

They haven't enough financial resources to fund even a tiny drop in the ocean of the amount of care families like ours really need. They have a real need to justify not spending too much money on things, such as carers in the home or an overnight respite stay, and the easiest way of doing that is to deny that the pressures you are under are really as bad as all that. This has the added insult of making you feel even less able and competent than you really are, and you can easily start to think that every other mother coping with children like yours is managing so much better than you are, and that really, you're just bordering on incompetent.

Once you start feeling like this, you become even more reluctant to ask for help, because you don't want your shortcomings highlighted so obviously. It becomes a vicious circle, you can barely cope, but you can't ask for help because you think they think you should be coping better, so without the help you cope even less well.... and so it goes on.

So I would walk into discussions already mentally exhausted, and then I would feel I had to wind my neck right back in and not to be so obviously needy and lacking as a human being. These professionals, particularly en masse, have the ability to patronise right down to a fine art. You very quickly can err towards paranoia and start to worry that, if they think you are as hopeless as that as a parent, you could lose your kids.

Without realising, I was helping them to achieve their objectives of protecting their budgets. Even now, I still struggle with asking for help because it does feel like I'm admitting defeat.

If I had had a better understanding of the definition of stress, which is basically the difference between what you are expected to achieve, and your available resources to easily achieve these expectations, I would have been able to present a more reasoned, rational and less emotionally-charged argument in those early days.

I do clearly remember one very defining moment. My marriage was falling apart, and my husband and I were spending long periods apart to try and find a way forward, so effectively I was already a single mother for a lot of the time.

Francesca crawled onto my lap and hugged me tightly and I realised that she, too, was picking up much too much of the stress. I looked at her, then I looked at Toby and it suddenly hit me that if I went under, they would too. I resolved there and then that come what may, for their sakes, I simply could never let that happen. All this crying I had been doing simply had to stop. This wasn't about me, this was about them. Furthermore, I resolved that this being their only shot at childhood, they both deserved the very best, and that they also deserved a happy, cheerful and fully involved mother, the very best mother I could possibly be.

There have been many days since when I've had to pretend like crazy, and it's a bit of an in-joke that my demeanour throughout their childhood was along the lines of a rather over-exaggerated pre-school TV presenter, overly jolly and jumping around and singing loudly in an off-key slightly oddball way most of the time, but generally I hope all three of my children would remember having a very happy childhood despite being part of a quirky, unconventional household by default. We focused on fun, and we had a lot of it together at home, punctuated by moments of sheer terror while Toby struggled to breathe or whatever, but mostly it was good.

Friends and family, like my lovely close-knit band of young-mother neighbours, all rallied around and turned up and did what they could, but I wasn't able to direct them properly, I was too tired, and too guilt-ridden to get them to really support me in the things I wasn't able to do. Francesca was being farmed out far too often when Toby was in hospital and she was becoming withdrawn and traumatised as a result, so by the time Toby was a few weeks old she would join us in that cramped little side room every time he was hospitalised. She was amazing, she learnt very quickly not to touch the leads and lines that led into and out of his body and to keep very quiet when doctors came to see us. There were huge plusses too though, she had more stories read to her and nursery rhymes sung to her than most children ever do – somehow Toby's situation was creating quality time for me to respond to both my small children, and Francesca's speech, reading and writing were assessed as being a year ahead when she started school at 5.

Family and friends can help out in the short term, or during real emergencies, but it is hard to expect that sort of on-going commitment year after year. My lovely Dad, who is now in his eighties, and my caring sister have never let me down – even now if I need them they turn up at a moment's notice whatever the time of day or night.

Over time my resilience increased and I learnt to plough deeply for resources I didn't know I had. Slowly but surely, I got better at coping with the demands of Toby's condition and juggling everything else too.

Sometimes I used to get overwhelmed with anger and resentment, not at the children, but at the rest of the world. Friends and relatives doing normal things like watching a movie on TV or going to the cinema or out for a meal, that sort of thing. This awfulness was happening in my family behind our closed doors and the rest of the world was still turning as if nothing had happened.

I now understand that change is normal, it can happen, anytime and to anybody, and it often has far-reaching consequences. I also know that life is unpredictable, stuff happens at random, and none of us can protect ourselves from that. Accepting change and being able to go with it instead of resisting it makes it all a thousand times easier, another big life lesson I've learnt along the way.

In the early days, changes were happening so quickly and I was under so much pressure to keep Toby's punishingly difficult health care plan going that I was just reacting to events, rather than being proactive. Reactive responses make one feel powerless and impotent. Over time, I learnt to wriggle little bits and pieces of control back into our lives, and became much more proactive, which is very empowering and helps to maintain both dignity and confidence in a way that both those qualities of mine were just washed away in the early days.

Hindsight is fantastic, and I can now look back and see a load of things I could and should have done differently, but we can only do the best we can with the resources we have and the knowledge we know at any given time.

I did learn some strategies to cope. The ten minute chunks of time taken a chunk at a time made everything seem much more bearable and doable, but then I learnt another. When everything was just beyond me, when I was furious with life and holding back the tears all the time, I invented the "Thirty Minute Wallow". It was so effective. I'd set the alarm for half an hour, and during that time I could scream, cry, throw paperbacks at the front door all the way down the hall, rant, rave, whatever as long as it was productively cathartic. Then when the alarm went off, I'd make myself a nice cup of tea and the world looked a whole load better. Obviously, the children were safely tucked up and fast asleep before I could wallow, but those wallow periods were something else I started to look forward to when the going got really tough.

The other thing I learnt were that certain emotions are a completely draining, pointless waste of time. Worry is one of them. Either something bad is going to happen or it isn't. If it does happen, you'll need all your wits about you, and have enough energy to make the very best of it. If you have squandered all your energy resources in worrying about it, you'll be hopeless at sorting things out when that bad thing actually happens. Or if it never happens, what on earth was the point of spending all that time feeling miserable and helpless by wasting it all on worry?

Guilt is another. All you ever do when you beat yourself up over something that is well in the past and can't be changed is that you drain all your mental reserves of strength and emotional energy. I was constantly feeling that I somehow could and should be doing things better, faster, more efficiently..... looking back I can see I was strung out, exhausted, over-worked and doing much more than anyone should ever have expected of me, and doing it pretty well too.

I wish I'd taken some time to step back and look at the situation and take stock properly. I juggled far too much for far too long and I should have asked for help sooner, or used help more constructively when it was offered.

I should have made more of an effort to hold onto certain friends who fell by the wayside, and found the courage to dump others who just made me feel worse.

I should have realised that I couldn't expect anyone to really understand the pressure and stress I was under – this was such an extreme situation that expecting people to "get it" was asking way too much of most people, professionals included.

One thing I luckily did master fairly early on was putting a bright face on things. I probably did it for the wrong reasons, to make people believe that I was fine and coping and taking things in my stride when I clearly wasn't, but it still made things much much easier. Nobody likes a whinge-bag, and I'm sure if I had moaned and groaned and been thoroughly miserable all the time I would have lost a lot of friends and not retained the goodwill that still gets extended to me and my family time and time and time again.

However, it is important to acknowledge those negative feelings, which I don't think I was good enough at doing. Perhaps someone to talk to outside of the situation might have helped. Looking back, I think I probably had to keep on kidding even myself that everything was hunky dory and manageable, or I might have gone under too.

Linking up with other special parents

One thing that really helped was being invited to join a support network of other mothers with their very young disabled children. Every week, a taxi would turn up and take us off to a local play-centre, and when we arrived the children would be taken from us to play in a fabulously well-resourced playroom, with very highly skilled medical staff caring for them. Meanwhile all the mums went into a lovely living room with sink-deeply-into-and-almost-disappear sofas, given cups of tea and unlimited chocolate biscuits, and a trained facilitator would gently lead us to sharing the previous week's news about our fragile and broken-feeling families.

Some of those other mums have become life-long friends. We shared tears, hopes, dreams, disasters, triumphs and successes, and no matter how low we felt on arrival, by the end of the afternoon we always found something to laugh at until it hurt.

That was the start of building a new friendship group that has held me together through thick and thin – the "special parents" I know so well. Once upon a time I had never met anyone who had a disabled child, now I hardly know anyone who doesn't. Universally we "get it" and that is so life-enhancingly reassuring. Get any bunch of special mums or dads together, and you won't be able to speak for laughing so hard. It is often gallows humour in very poor taste, but there is such a rich vein of hilarity in all of our peculiar lives that it's infectious and great fun.

Other parents are also the very best source of information that there is – they know the best specialists, the best schools, how to get the right therapy for your child, how to apply for funding for this, that and the other. When things are going badly, or you just hit a bad day when nothing feels good and you don't think it ever will again, the other special parents are the ones who understand without you having to explain anything, and they are the ones who can pull you out of the emotional mud faster than anybody else.

Finances

There are likely to be huge financial implications on the family purse due to all sorts of things. Generally speaking, it's very hard for both parents to continue to work full-time when there is a child with so many extra needs to care for, so income is likely to be significantly reduced while outgoings are escalating.

In 2012 Contact a Family conducted a survey entitled: "Counting the Costs, the financial reality for families with disabled children in the UK". The findings showed that a disabled child costs around 7 times as much to raise as a non-disabled child does. One in six families were found to be going without food, one in five families were going without heating, and nearly one-third were only making ends meet by taking out loans to cover costs, often essential costs like utility bills. A quarter of these loans were from quick cash schemes or loan sharks. Many families also reported the sense of shame and stigma on being reliant on benefits.

There are UK benefits that your child may be eligible to receive, currently Disability Living Allowance, although this is shortly to be changed to a Personal Independence Payment, and the changeover is predicted to be likely to adversely affect many families financially. Even if your child is awarded the highest rate of these benefits, it nowhere near covers the difference in costs.

There are charities and organisations that may fund one-off items, and there is also a thriving second-hand market for specialist equipment and toys, but many families have to make huge sacrifices, and accept that they will be surviving on a severely reduced income for the foreseeable future.

Certainly in the early years, we lived on or very close to the breadline. Over the years money-management has become an essential skill to acquire. Every penny has to be spent wisely, there can never be impulse-buy moments, extravagant purchases or designer-anything. Ours is very much a household of make-do-and-mend, and a keen eye for discounts and bargains. There are no rainy-day savings. I have never had credit cards, if the money isn't there it isn't bought, I cannot afford to get into any sort of debt whatsoever. Food shopping is done with extreme care, even taking into account the eating issues and special diets in my household, waste has to be minimised on every level. Clothes are worn until they are falling apart, then sewn back together and worn again. It isn't always easy, but it is the only way we have survived. The one thing I have learned to do is to accept it, not to waste time or energy in feeling upset about it, and just getting on with keeping costs as low as we possibly can.

TIPS, TRICKS AND STRATEGIES

These are things I didn't know then, but I wish I had

I would have worked out what my limitations and boundaries were, and then moved heaven and earth to fill the edges beyond those limitations and boundaries with help, either from the Statutory Services or from friends and relatives, but in a much more structured way.

I would have made sure I didn't get lost in the relentlessness of it all. I would have worked out what things made me happy and were the essence of "me", and I would have been doggedly determined to carve out time to do those things. For me, it would have been going out for a meal, sharing a bottle of wine with an old friend, going to the theatre or cinema for a whole evening off, or just sitting quietly and reading a good book. I should have ensured I had at least one whole evening off a month, having something good to look forward to would have made all the difference.

I would have found a way to take control, even of small, little things, much much sooner.

I'd have found some special parents to share experiences with much earlier, they have been the reason I'm still vaguely sane, able to laugh, and have learnt to cope with most things life has thrown at me. They are better than any medicine, they understand the place I'm coming from and I understand their difficulties too. To find that level of understanding and empathy is priceless.

I would have tried to take a "bigger picture" approach, being better able to understand how shock can knock you off balance and destabilise you. I couldn't grasp that I was actually coping very well indeed, instead I continually felt that I wasn't quite doing well enough, and that I was failing all over the place. I allowed my confidence to evaporate, and I felt intimidated, judged and back-footed, when I should have been incredibly proud of what I was actually achieving.

I wish I'd invented my own strategies much sooner – the 10 minute chunks and the 30 minute wallow made a huge difference in being able to cope with what was, quite frankly, the impossible.

I wish I'd believed in the future and not wasted so much time worrying myself sick about things that never happened. I now know that, whatever the future holds, it will never be as bad as you imagine it will be, and you will have the resources and resilience to cope with it all, and an ability to take it in your stride. In my case, all three of my children have come further than anyone would have believed possible. The future really does take care of itself.

CHAPTER 5
Building your Support Network

You can get through anything if you have the right people around you, pulling together. An ideal support network is made up of friends, neighbours, family and other parents going through similar things. If you can, get to know and trust one or two of the professionals on your child's team so that they can become part of your support network too.

The right professionals on-board can act as a very good sounding-board, they'll have a good overview of your child's situation, and also a broader picture of how the dynamics work within the team of professionals supporting your child. Before you reveal anything, though, ask that it's an "off the record" discussion, because professionals often feel they have to record every conversation they have with you. It's not helpful if your every wobbly "what do I do next" moment is recorded in detailed reports for posterity, so that any professional now or in the future can access a file and make the wrong assumptions about you and your family.

It also helps if you bear in mind that your closest friends and family care deeply for you and yours, and they are probably also trying to come to terms with the difficult news of your child's condition. They may be trying to protect you from their feelings and therefore may be accidentally coming across perhaps as different in some way, maybe distant or aloof, or overly jocular and relentlessly cheerful. This can lead to all sorts of misunderstandings and communication breakdowns if it isn't recognised and corrected quickly by straight-talking and open discussion.

There may be others who just overwhelm you with their own sadness about the situation. It's hard enough to be handling your own emotions without taking on responsibility for other people's feelings too. It's lovely that they care, but you may find it all very draining and exhausting having them around you too much. There are times you may just feel the need to be alone with your own sorrows without having to acknowledge those of other people. Without a doubt, all my friendships and relationships were gradually reassessed over a period of time, and many good friendships fell by the wayside. In return, though, there have been some really positive surprises, when I have found unexpected support and understanding from people I considered only as acquaintances.

It also helps if you can work out the sort of help you really need, and how to best achieve it. This is something I'm totally hopeless at! People come over when they know I'm struggling to offer "help". I'm too polite to actually give them an unpleasant task to do when they get here, because I'm so grateful that they have turned up. Instead I do everything myself, as well as make umpteen extra cups of tea and even cooking meals for several people while they chat and laugh together and have a great time, but still I feel indebted to them for giving up their precious time to "help".

It's a bit of a family joke now, and these "help" sessions have become a bit of a regular drop in session for loads of people every Friday night and Sunday afternoon, with very little actual "help" ever materialising. Later into the evening, it suddenly occurs to me that there were loads of jobs I could have asked them to do; filing, filling in forms, popping to the shops, tidying the toys, mending the broken ones....but by then everyone's far too relaxed, deep in conversation or raucous laughter, and the moment has gone.

Over the years, though, everyone has, at one time or another, really pulled out all the stops to help in times of real trouble. I just sometimes still need to learn to work out what sort of help I really need before they arrive rather than just when they're about to leave.

Things I should ask myself are things like this. For instance, how easy is it to get to the shops? In my case in the early days it was really difficult, and I'm a cup-of-tea addict, so running out of milk is always a disaster.

How well do you know your neighbours, and are any of them in all day? Get to know them, be friendly, and if they are going out to the shops anyway, hopefully they won't mind doing a small favour when they are out. I had two rules: never ask them to pick up more than 2 items, and always give them the money in advance.

How complex are your child's needs? Is there anyone in your circle who would be willing to learn about their needs so that they could become competent to care for them occasionally? There will always be times you will need to go to the doctor or dentist for yourself or one of your other children, or rush around the shops, or even to ensure you have back-up to stop you going completely stir-crazy. Sometimes, just another responsible adult in the house to share the load for an hour or two is a godsend.

In Toby's case, due to his tendency to stop breathing or become life-threateningly ill at a moment's notice, there wasn't exactly a queue of brave volunteers prepared to take on the responsibility. However both my Dad and my sister became very competent at all the aspects of his care, and were able to let me off the hook at reasonably regular intervals.

What about care for your other children if things with your special child escalate suddenly? I lived in a little cul-de-sac where nearly all my neighbours had small children, and we had already formed a very tight-knit friendship group by the time Toby was born, with our children virtually growing up together. I was so lucky, because they were always happy to look after Francesca at a moment's notice, pick up shopping, or just come over and put the kettle on.

Take stock of who you know locally, do you have any close friends on the doorstep, or are there any families with small children living on your road, who you may have noticed but haven't really started to get to know yet? It is worth making the first steps towards a friendship with them, maybe starting by just waving when you see them, then stopping for a quick chat, and see where that takes you.

Often local church halls or children's centres have drop in sessions for mothers and small children. For us, with Toby's very precarious health, it wasn't possible to join in with these sorts of groups very often, but occasionally when I did manage it we all had a great time.

Friendship is reciprocal. What can you offer in return for practical help? Sometimes all I was able to offer was a cup of tea and an hour to chat while I still worked on Toby's health regime, but that has turned out to be as good a basis as any for the start of a friendship.

Social Media is also a really great tool for keeping in touch. I wish Facebook had been invented when Toby was little. I use it all the time now, and it is so easy to let people know you're still thinking about them and still care about their friendship when it only takes a moment or two. In the old days, the only way to keep in touch was by long, intense weekly phone-calls or meeting up and spending time together or going out. I didn't have time to do any of that. You keep meaning to pick up the phone and talk to someone, but days, then weeks, then months go by without having done it, and you start to feel embarrassed. Even worse, if they ring you and catch you at a bad moment and you promise to ring back but you just never get round to it. Facebook solves all those dilemmas.

On Facebook you can also often find a specific page leading you to other parents facing similar challenges to your own. Most medical conditions have Facebook pages where families can virtually meet and exchange stories and experiences. Online generally there are also forums specially set up for parents like us to chat to others in a similar boat. It helps so much to reduce the feelings of isolation that parents of disabled children so often experience. It's easier to find people facing similar problems these days than ever before, and it's really helpful when you do.

If you are offered any support groups, just make yourself go. Even if you are reticent about it at first, the most vital piece of advice I can pass on to any other parent of a disabled child is find other local parents facing similar predicaments. If you see another parent with a disabled child in the hospital or GP's waiting room or even If you see a parent pushing a wheelchair around the supermarket, say hello. Find ways to reach out to this group of parents in any way you can. A friend of a friend may have a child with difficulties, if so, ask for an introduction, or talk to the professionals you are involved with – do they know any other parents who may be coping with similar issues?

It doesn't matter if their children's conditions are completely different to your child's, or if their children are several years older or younger. These parents will keep you going through the worst and the best of times regardless. They instantly "get it". The fatigue, the concerns, the frustrations, the sadnesses; if the road to friendship starts from having things in common, you are already a mile down that road with other special parents. The information they can tell you about local services, various professionals, which venues are great at accommodating your child and which others don't even try, schools, clubs, and how to access things. Like many thousands of parents in our situation I have learnt far more, far quicker, from talking to other parents than I have ever learnt from talking to the professionals.

These are people with whom you can completely let your hair down. You can turn up at their houses with your child and no matter what their disability is or how they behave or what they do, there is never a need to apologise or feel embarrassed. They just understand on a really deep level in a way that other people can't grasp unless they've lived it too. Other parents can come up with practical solutions reached by trial and error that nobody else would ever have thought of, or if they can't they can pour you another glass of wine instead. They can help you find a funny-side to things that have been driving you half-mad, and intuitively, they just know when you need a hug or a shoulder to cry on. With other parents like us, there are very few "off-topic" subjects, so there's none of that glazed embarrassed pity from people who really can't think of anything to say, and are so frightened of saying something that might upset you that they say nothing until the subject can safely be changed.

These other parents who simply "get it" will also have you laughing until tears roll, which is a far better way of dealing with our demons than being miserable about everything.

On Facebook, I successfully combine the three; social media, special parents and shockingly irreverent humour. People add comments over several days sometimes, just getting funnier and funnier, until it could almost be sold as a script for a sitcom, except it would probably never be aired because the humour is in such appallingly bad taste. The humour is normally around the ridiculous situations we find ourselves in, the absurdity of some of the meetings we have to endure, or the reactions of other people towards our children.

There are other sorts of help you might need too. Your admin mountain is probably beginning to reach epic proportions. Can someone help to file it all? You may have to pick the right person; a lot of it is confidential, and if it includes award notices of any state benefits or other financial matters you may not want everyone to know all your business. However, very close and trusted friends or relatives can really take the pressure off by rolling up their sleeves and just getting on with it.

Can anyone help you fill out all the mindless forms that seem to go with the territory of disability? You won't know if you don't ask. What about housework? I used to hate the idea of even asking other people to help with the cleaning, but I've been amazed at how many people I know actually seem to enjoy being able to do something practical to help, and also, how they put me to shame with their speed and efficiency at household chores. However, it's still a rare treat; I'm not so shameless that I could sit back and let my friends do all my housework.

Try and think about what aspects of your daily life that you really are struggling with, or even the bits of it that you are growing to loathe. I got to the point whereby I absolutely hated giving Toby his nebulisers. There were so many to give during the day, it took so long and it was so noisy that I really became irrationally irritated by the task. So if anyone was in the house when one was due, I used to set it all up, plonk Toby on their lap and ask them to do it while I escaped to the kitchen and had a chat with the kettle.

Then try and think who might be good at helping with which tasks. You really don't want to set them up to fail, or have to take over halfway through which might shatter their confidence.

Another really important task that often gets forgotten is to have some people around you who can just help you retain your own sense of identity. It's so easy to get so sucked into the needs of everybody else and get into a routine where you're just running around catching your tail, so it's good to have friends and family who can still touch base with who you really are.

Hold on to old friends if you can. Nowadays I really value the handful of people who have known me since before Toby came along, people who knew me when I wasn't just "Toby's Mum". Something I've always been acutely aware of is how other people's perceptions change when they know I have children with disabilities, particularly when one of them is as severely disabled as Toby.

People mean well and say genuinely lovely things, but sometimes, when you're feeling a bit overwrought and sensitive, even the most sincere of compliments can feel like slings and arrows. I've learnt to listen to their intention rather than their words, it's usually very apparent that they so want to say something that will help, and it's just not fair to reject a good intention because they picked the wrong words or delivered them in a clumsy way.

I'm always pleased when people try to say anything at all about our situation, at least they are trying to reach out and cross the invisible bridge that sometimes seems as if it is separating us from everybody else. The worst is when people don't even try to connect.

People will tell you how marvellous you are, or how amazing you're being, or how they could never, in a million years, do what you're having to do every day.

What they can't be expected to appreciate is that being told that you're somehow different, even if that difference is presented as complimentary, can in itself feel very isolating. It can remind you of how very different your own life is becoming, highlighting the fact that other people see you as being apart in some way. People may think we're flattered to be told we are inspiring and amazing and wonderful, when all we really want to feel is that we're the same as everyone else. We don't always want to be reminded of how our new lifestyle is pushing us to the outer edges of what feels "normal". So sometimes when someone says "You are amazing" we actually hear "You're not the same as the rest of us".

However, I know people mean well, and they say these things with such warmth and care which I really appreciate. One of the joys of parenting children like mine is that I've seen time and again how most people really do have very kind hearts, and even complete strangers are mostly very considerate. Despite all we read in the press about negative public reactions towards disability, that has not been my experience at all.

There have only been two moments when I have actually been crushed to the core by things strangers have said to me. One was an insensitive young mother who told me it was fine for Toby to have needles stuck into him because he must be used to it by now, but for her little boy it was heartbreakingly awful. The other was an old lady in a supermarket who peered into Toby's pram and recoiled in horror when she saw tubes coming out of his face, then started to shout abuse at me along the lines that I had no right to leave the house with him because he was so disgusting.

Both incidents happened before Toby was a year old, and both cut me to the very core, leaving me floored emotionally for days on end.

I think the world has moved on a tremendous amount since both those moments, the degree of tolerance and acceptance towards disability has increased beyond measure since the mid-nineties and I doubt either incident would occur in quite the same way now. However, I really wish I hadn't got myself so upset about both situations. There was plenty enough going on in my daily existence to cause upset, I wish I had then had the skills I've developed since not to let other people's ignorance ruin my day.

It may help to accept that perhaps you feel too raw and vulnerable to cope in certain situations and to let other people know that you just can't manage certain things at the moment.

I had a lot of friends with babies of a similar age to Toby. They would come over to our house, and be so proud of their babies' latest achievements like clapping hands, or crawling, or eating solids, or saying their first words. I wanted to be happy for them, I really did, but it tore me in two. It took a lot of effort to say the right things and be encouragingly supportive while hiding the hurt I felt at having the contrast between where Toby was and where he should have been developmentally highlighted so vividly.

If you're anything like me, there may be times when people do or say things that sometimes seem annoying, but if you can, try and relax and find a funny side. I've been on the receiving end of countless pieces of unsolicited advice or homespun philosophising, but generally people mean well. Extended family in particular sometimes seem to have a knack of overstepping the mark with their "helpful" comments, but learning to take it in your stride rather than boiling up in seething anger every time is a skill well worth perfecting. Smiling sweetly, and just saying "Thank you, I'll bear that in mind" can work wonders. There's no point getting upset. They are family, they care and they really are trying to help even if it comes out wrong. Deep down, they want the best for all of you and it's very hard for them to watch you struggle while they feel powerless to make things better.

TIPS, TRICKS AND STRATEGIES

Surround yourself with happy, supportive people you like and who are willing to help, build a team of friends and family who you can count on.

Encourage at least some of these friends to become confident enough to be able to care for your children on their own.

Start to reach out to other parents of disabled children, particularly if they are local.

Use Social Media such as Facebook to stay in touch with friends, and forums to meet other families of disabled children in similar situations.

Be honest with people, if you aren't feeling up to certain situations, don't do them.

Find ways of diluting the difficult moments with humour.

Remember people generally mean well and their hearts are in the right place.

Ask for help – people may actually want to be able to help in some way.

Be aware of how people make you feel when you're with them. Some people seem to bring extra energy into your life, others seem to drain you of all your resources. Find ways to reduce the negative effects of these people, either by reducing contact with them for the time being, or by trying to find another way to view them that may minimise their effect on you.

Find people with whom you can always be yourself.

If you can, try and hold on to and cherish those old friends who knew you before you became a "special parent". These are the people who will always help you find the essence of who you really are and who will help you let your hair down and be yourself. From this point on, it's very easy for other people to define you as simply "that poor child's parent", and sometimes you can feel that you are losing your identity. Old friends who are good friends will remember who you really are, and over the years they become as valuable as gold.

CHAPTER 6
Your Child

Right at the heart of everything is your child, the very focus of your life, and hopefully, your love. Some parents feel very far away from loving their child when everything around them seems so unstable, whereas others immediately feel fierce protective overwhelming feelings of love towards their child, and there are many parents who veer between the two extremes.

Your child, even if they are still a very young baby, will be picking up on the emotional environment their parents are creating around them. If they are a little bit older, they may well have heard and understood things that could be playing on their mind and perhaps frightening them. It is so important to let them know about their own condition and the possible consequences of it, but how you tell them is also incredibly important.

It's a tall order, I know, at a time when you may be feeling crushed and devastated, to find a way to talk to the very child at the centre of all of this in a way that is upbeat, positive, sensitive and empowering, but there is no alternative. The way in which a child learns that they have some form of disability, medical condition or special needs will have a significant impact on how they feel about themselves forever. Self-confidence and self-esteem are at the core of how we, as human beings, relate to the world, and our children especially need an abundance of both if they are to grow and develop to become well-rounded, balanced young adults who are capable of living their lives, however restricted, to the full.

If they have heard things in a way that was inappropriate or upsetting to them, or if they have overheard snippets of adult conversation about what's going on, it's not the end of the world, but it's very helpful if you can carry out some damage limitation and find ways to get a positive outlook back on track.

Disability is not the end of the world. We each only have one life, and every life is worth living and enjoying. Although it can be sad that your child may not be able to do certain things that others take for granted, there are still many opportunities open for your child, even though in the early stages it may not feel as if there are. I see my parenting role as encouraging my children to paint their lives on as broad a canvas as they possibly can, despite their disabilities. I have always encouraged them to live life to the brim and to be as happy and fulfilled as they can be while they are doing it.

Find out as much as you can about their medical condition or disability, seek out support groups or charities working with families like yours, and find something positive about these children's abilities and achievements to hold on to. If you feel it may help, get a referral to a psychologist who may be able to encourage your child to explore their feelings and come to terms with their newly-diagnosed "label". Some families have also benefitted enormously from family therapy at times like this, where everyone in the family can talk openly about how disability is affecting them, in a safe, supportive environment where the family dynamic can be looked at and strengthened.

Your child may have a disability, but they are still a child, and they deserve a childhood as rich in experience and fun as any other. It's sometimes easy to lose sight of this aspect, when their medical care is so overwhelming and their disabilities are affecting a whole range of aspects of their life. But who they are and the adult they will become is much more important than the set of words bestowed upon your family by the medical profession to describe your child's condition.

The world may try and label your child, but one of your tasks from now on is to help your child step out from behind that label and show the world who they really are. Like every other child on this planet, they will have the capacity to both warm hearts and drive their parents to the brink of frustration, but they will also have talents, characteristics, likes and dislikes that form their very own unique personality.

Toby may resemble a two year old in his cognitive abilities, and can test the patience of a saint when he's got a bee in his bonnet, but he gives the best hugs and can blow the best kisses in the whole wide world, and he also has the ability to collect people who quickly adore him wherever he goes. My other two continually inspire and amaze me as they go from strength to strength, taking life by the horns and totally living it.

Our job as parents is to find the essence of who our child is, never forgetting that their disability is only a string of words and it doesn't have to define every aspect of their lives. It's up to you to discover what they can do rather than focusing on what they can't achieve.

Sometimes, their disabilities make exploring and experiencing the world much harder than for most children, and therefore they aren't necessarily picking up the early life lessons that most families take for granted for their children. For instance, a child with mobility problems won't have the knocks and scrapes, falls and bumped heads that naturally help shape a toddler's understanding of gravity, balance, solid objects and spatial awareness. If a child can never jump in a puddle, it will take them longer to learn about the properties of water. So if you can, use your imagination to bring those experiences to your child. I often had bowls of water on the floor near Toby for him to dangle his hands in and splash. I'd hold him up high and together we would drop a ball to the floor. There are dozens of hands-on ways that you can actually both have a lot of fun while helping your child to engage with life-lesson moments.

However, you do want your child to grow into an adult with a reasonable skill-set of acceptable behaviour, manners and social skills. That means that, in childhood, you have to set boundaries and expectations, something many parents of disabled children find very difficult to do.

The usual advice found in parenting manuals simply doesn't always fit our children. You'll have to throw the manuals away and write some new guidelines all of your own, then see if they'll work. However, before you do that, you have to ask yourself some questions, and be clear in your own mind what your own values are, what values you want to pass on to your child, and how best to help them understand why good behaviours are important.

There really isn't much advice around for parents like us. I've found it useful to be clear in my mind that there are two very different types of negative behaviour; whether something is just going to be annoying and create extra work like deliberately spilling a drink, or if someone is likely to get hurt, like a child picking up a heavy object to hurl at their brother's head.

The responses to each again are different. I have a particular warning screech intended to shock and distract the child for long enough to intervene in dangerous situations, and a much more gentle, patient approach for the annoying moments.

With children like ours, it isn't about punishment or sanctions. I've found it's all got to be done very calmly and patiently, demonstrating good behaviours and minimising the less good ones.

For example, Toby loves making people laugh, and enjoys being the centre of attention. When he has done something wrong, I use an exaggerated sad, long face to show I'm not happy, and hope against hope that everyone else in the room will follow suit. I also try, as far as possible, to let him deal with the consequences of his behaviour, for instance, he has to help wipe up any spillages or help tidy any messes he has made.

This isn't easy when he has a three-second attention span and is very clever at turning everything he possibly can into a game. Even if it is only the most cursory single flick of a dishcloth at a mess, though, he has to do it.

I also use a lot of praise and applause for when I "catch" him doing something right. He just loves a round of applause, and this sort of thing works really well, but it has to be consistent, and very long-term; there are areas of behaviour I'm still working on ten years after starting.

The other thing I try to remember is that all behaviour is communication. Toby cannot talk, other than a few simple words, so sometimes his only way to let people know that they are annoying him is to lash out physically at them. If he hurts someone, it's never acceptable, but it is worth bearing in mind that he doesn't have the ability that other children and young people have of giving verbal warnings of his increasing irritation or annoyance with people.

Sometimes it's easier to use pictures than words, and social stories, in particular, can be very helpful.

Social stories tell a story about a situation which can be adapted to be relevant for your own child and your family situation, maybe using their own name as the star of the story, with their brothers' and sisters' names being used for supporting characters. These stories are very simple, and deal with concepts very clearly, and you can read them over and over again to reinforce the message. They can deal with single-issue behaviours like hitting a sibling or pulling all the books off a shelf and spreading them around on the floor, and they can be very effective if used properly.

Sensory stories, too, are very effective. These are stories where there are lots of opportunities for the child to experience things through their senses, particularly sound, sight and touch. So if rain features in the story, you can have a bowl of water to encourage your child to flick some drops from his hand to recreate rain, or if there is a loud bang in the story, your child could hit an upturned saucepan with a wooden spoon at the appropriate moment.

If you can combine the two elements of social and sensory factors within the same story about a single issue behaviour message, and repeat the story with both of you having fun in the retelling of it, the child has a much better chance of understanding these messages and taking them on board much more quickly.

I also sing a lot. That was something that developed early on, and sometimes Toby seemed to understand and take on concepts if they were sung rather than spoken. Some years later I discovered that there are actually scientific reasons as to why this may be so, because words that are sung to music and the spoken word are processed by different parts of our brains.

Once I understood this, I developed the singing even further, and I often sing instructions to him, which is very effective, particularly if I can sing them to the same tune as a song or nursery rhyme he knows well.

For instance, the following words fit beautifully to the same tune as "The Grand Old Duke of York":-

"Grandad needs a hug, because his head now hurts,
Because you threw a book at him, and that wasn't very nice".

Yes, sometimes I feel very silly indeed, but if it works, that's all that matters!

Saying sorry is non-negotiable, and he now knows to say and sign the word for "sorry" at the right time, while looking appropriately sheepish.

Pleases and thank-yous are also non-negotiable, although they have taken years to establish properly, and please is still very hit and miss with Toby. However, he has learnt excellent "meet and greet" skills when people come over to our house, opening the door, giving them a hug, helping them off with their coat and bringing their arrival to my attention. These skills and behaviours have been taught over many years, although some things, the things Toby enjoys like the meeting and greeting, are significantly easier to establish than others.

We also all learnt the very basic sign language developed especially for children with learning disabilities or speech difficulties. Toby understands it perfectly, although he chooses not to use it himself most of the time, but it has bridged a gap in communication on a number of occasions. Certainly, it helps to underline a behavioural concept. Pictures work really well too, the first one I managed to establish with any success was a picture of the palm side of a hand, to signify "STOP".

When I speak to Toby, I only talk in very short sentences, four or five words at a time. I speak slowly and clearly, and ensure I have his full attention and that he is looking at me. I will often repeat the same sentence three or four times before moving on to the next sentence. Toby struggles to understand, and I see it as my job to do everything I can to help him communicate by whatever means possible, using a combination of speech, signing, pictures and singing. Even though he is largely non-verbal, we normally get there in the end and he can use the same methods to communicate his needs and wants too. It can take a lot of patience and it's important to stay very calm and cheerful, but it works.

With children like ours, there are difficulties in implementing any form of behaviour strategy that just doesn't occur anywhere to the same extent with other children.

When there is a fragile child with a serious illness or disability in the family, the overwhelming tendency is to be protective and loving towards that child. Sometimes, no, actually quite often, this tendency can cross the line and become over-indulgent, and you find yourself letting the child off the hook for transgressions, and before long, the child is being thoroughly spoiled.

Children with disabilities learn very early on how to get adults completely wrapped around their little fingers. They can be utterly shameless in their ability to turn on the cute charm whenever the need arises, and when they know they have overstepped the mark, my goodness, they can be absolute masterminds at emotional manipulation.

There are times when I am completely determined to indicate disappointment and displeasure about a particular moment of Toby's poor behaviour. I'll pull a very long, serious and sad face, and talk to him in a tone of admonishment. However, he will simultaneously be equally determined to do everything in his power to ensure I dissolve into fits of giggles. It's his hopelessly cute butter-wouldn't-melt-in-his-mouth innocent look that he gives me, coupled with his fired-up sense of humour shining brightly from his eyes, as he does everything he can think of to make me laugh. Guess who normally wins?!

It can also be really difficult to get the rest of your family and friends to support you in your behaviour strategy attempts. Mostly they subscribe to the "poor little mite" school of undermining you. It's particularly annoying when you are trying to convey a behavioural message, and a family member rushes towards Toby, takes him in their arms in a flamboyant hug, and tells you how he didn't mean it, he couldn't help it and that you're being a bit too hard on him.

However, there may be one or two others, equally irritating, but taking the opposite view. They give the impression that they regard you as the softest, most ineffectual parent ever, and they are award-winning experts at giving the most tactless pieces of unsolicited advice at precisely the moment where it will best hit you on a raw nerve.

To be honest, hardly anyone will understand what you are trying to achieve and how you are aiming to do it. You can try and explain what your thinking is until you're blue in the face, but often, blanket disapproval of your behaviour strategy attempts is virtually universal. You can do what I tend to do and get really wound up and cross, or you can be a better person and let it flow away right over your head instead. Getting your extended family to all sing from the same song-sheet on this is virtually impossible.

Whenever you get a group of "special parents" together and chatting on this subject, you soon realise that every family has the same frustrations with their wider family. There is something about a child with disabilities that makes everyone feel they know best. You'll regularly feel undermined in your attempts to modify your child's behaviour because there is an overwhelming feeling from everyone that they want to protect and over-compensate that child for the tough set of cards that life has dealt them. If there is a behaviour moment that causes conflict between you and your child, your child will win the popularity contest from any stray visiting relatives around at the time, who won't be backwards in coming forwards to protect that poor little child from his mean parent who is telling him off.

Your extended family members aren't around all the time, and when they are there they only get a snapshot of your family dynamic. They won't back you or support you in any behaviour strategy towards your child because they simply find it very hard to believe that your precious little angel could ever do anything wrong.

It's annoying, frustrating and infuriating, but accept it, let it go, and just let it happen.

A lot of good behaviour has been reinforced by the effective use of distraction strategies at precisely the right moment. Sometimes you have to quickly jump on a new instance of mischievousness that might elicit a laugh from everyone to start with, but could also develop into a form of really bad behaviour if allowed to go unchecked. Noticing new behaviours and nipping them in the bud is crucial at times.

When dealing with behaviour issues, consistency is very important too, and if your child becomes very ill or has to cope with difficult or painful medical procedures, it can seem really tough to persevere on through with the same strategies while other things are going on.

However, if the strategies you are using are of the gentle guidance type, it really is helpful to continue with what you are working towards regardless of outside influences. Children need consistency, they need to know where they stand, and it can confuse them if boundaries are set in different places in different situations.

Another factor that parents like us must always bear in mind is that, sometimes, our child's behaviour is actually beyond their control. Children who have Autistic Spectrum Disorder diagnoses may have meltdowns, which can be extreme. Sanctions can be applied to temper tantrums, but not to meltdowns, and in chapter 16 we'll look at this issue more closely.

One of the challenges in parenting children like ours is knowing the difference between good, old-fashioned bad behaviour and things that they simply cannot control. I have sometimes got it wrong, but generally I've got there in the end. With all three of my children, there were some behaviours that I have just had to let pass under the radar, but there were also some behaviours they all understood pretty early on that are complete no-nos.

For me, there are some definite absolutes. These include kindness, consideration for others and basic good manners. I can honestly say that all three of my children have developed these basics in abundance.

My most effective parenting strategy so far has always been to be available for all three of them, to set good examples in the really important areas, and to create a happy atmosphere at home where they are able to talk about anything and where they actually want to pull together and co-operate as a team to the best of their abilities.

Sometimes, with behaviour, less is more. Jump on the really big things, and be prepared to turn a blind eye to lots of the little things. Step back, set a good example, make it clear how you expect things to be, and it works out roughly OK at least some of the time, which, considering the circumstances we've been given as a family, is more than enough for me.

TIPS, TRICKS AND STRATEGIES

Trust your instincts and listen to your child with all your senses, between you both you'll work most things out.

Your child is a child, and has the full range of "button-pressing" skills as much as any other child – just because they have disabilities doesn't mean they can't be naughty too!

Stick to your guns and don't let other people tell you you're doing it wrong. You are the only mum or dad ever to have brought up your particular children.

Work out what boundaries you want to set for your children, and then find your own way of helping your child recognise when they overstep them.

Use lots of praise, gentle guidance and repetition to help your child develop socially acceptable behaviour.

It will go wrong, there will be times when it will seem like you're not getting anywhere, so maybe take a break or try some new strategy. Basically, if one way isn't working, find another way.

Differentiate between annoying and dangerous behaviours, and develop ways to prevent injuries quickly.

Your child has a tougher road ahead than most of their peer-group, so the one attribute they will always need in abundance is self-confidence. Find ways to help your child develop their self-belief and self-esteem.

If it helps to know this, my three children, all on the brink of adulthood, are totally delightful and happy, and bring me more pride and joy than I once ever dared to expect.

CHAPTER 7
Siblings

What about your other children? It can be hard for any child to share Mummy and Daddy with a new baby brother or sister, but when that child arrives with the extra baggage of disability, it can be a total minefield of turmoil and confusion for everyone. Even tiny children pick up on some of what's going on in a way that often knocks the adults for six time and time again.

When Toby was born, Francesca was 18 months old. I had thought ahead and planned how to help her deal with a new interloper in the most positive way possible. One of the strategies I used was to buy her a lifelike baby doll, complete with nappies and bottles to feed it. I wrapped it up, took it into the hospital with me, and and left it in Toby's cot as a present from him to her, which she found when she came in to see us. It worked really well for a few weeks, and she and I would take care of our respective babies together.

However once Toby's hospital admissions began, the doll started being neglected and thrown around sometimes. The big issue seemed to be around feeding it – and the penny didn't drop with me until I found all her doll's baby bottles in the kitchen bin one day. Toby wasn't being fed by his mouth any more, he was being fed through a naso-gastric tube, so Francesca couldn't relate to her doll because it wasn't like her experience of a real baby.

An hour later, her baby had a long piece of string attached to its nose, with a small syringe that I'd painted white with correction fluid at the other end. Francesca immediately became the best little mummy in the world to her doll again, and she and I would sit together on the sofa holding our syringes of baby milk high in the air to feed our babies, who were sitting together in identical baby bouncers.

So even at less than 2 years old, Francesca had worked out something was wrong. She was beginning to speak, and among her first words were "Torticollis Physiotherapy", a procedure I had to do on Toby every day to help a tight muscle in his neck. Once we knew that he had Pseudo Bulbar Palsy, I explained it to Francesca that Toby had a "broken throat", which she completely took on board and became his little protector.

My children's grasp of the situation we were living in continually astonished me at times. Children understand much more than we give them credit for.

A few years later, when Adam had only been able to walk for a couple of months, I had left him and Toby watching a video while I prepared Toby's gastrostomy feed and Adam's lunch – the kitchen door was open so I could keep an eye on them throughout. Adam came out to the kitchen looking very serious and concerned. He kept saying "mouse". This was a new word, so I let him know how clever he was to tell me there was a mouse on the TV programme. But he became more insistent and started pulling me, "Mouse, mouse, mouse". So I took his hand and let him take me to have a look at whatever was worrying him. There was Toby, having put a small toy in his mouth, already blue and choking. Adam hadn't been saying "mouse" he'd been saying "mouth". At 18 months old he had already learned that anything in Toby's mouth was a serious danger, and he had the understanding to come and make me take notice.

There was another time when Francesca won an award from our local newspaper when she was only five, because she had saved Toby's life. Toby's choking episodes were a very common occurrence at home, as were the incidents when he would stop breathing altogether for no apparent reason. I had left Francesca and Toby together while I gave a newborn Adam a quick bath upstairs, and I asked Francesca to call me if Toby needed any help.

Toby stopped breathing while I was upstairs with Adam. Francesca called me immediately, but grabbing a wet baby and wrapping him in a towel takes a few seconds, as does running downstairs with him in my arms. Francesca already had Toby out of his chair and on the floor, rolled onto his side in the recovery position, and she was thumping his back with all her might – doing exactly what she had seen me do hundreds of times previously. Before I got to the bottom of the stairs he was coughing, and breathing safely again.

Like all brothers and sisters of seriously disabled children, both Francesca and Adam have made me proud beyond measure at times like this. The least I could do was to do my best to somehow create as normal a childhood as possible with fun factored in every day.

I realised very early on that Toby's care regime was so full-on that it would eat up every moment of every day if I let it, and that if I attended to his needs first the other two would never get a look-in. So I turned it upside down, and ensured that I always engaged the other two in absorbing tasks and giving them the attention they needed before starting a long chain of Toby's care. That meant not just dressing them and feeding them, but planning an activity that would keep them occupied and very close to me where I could see them while I had my hands full giving Toby his physiotherapy, nebulisers and a gastrostomy feed. Once you're holding a sick child on your lap with a nebuliser mask on his face, you really don't need a two-year old running around all over the house and possibly falling over and hurting themselves, so it was crucial that they were both under my nose where I could see them.

I bought Francesca a little second-hand desk which we put in the living room, and she loved it. She was very good, and would sit at it and paint, or do colouring, or make things, or play with stickers. However, she was so tiny, that her concentration didn't always last very long, so I would have to have a long repertoire of other things up my sleeve to keep her occupied. We often would sing every song we could think of for Toby, and he particularly loved watching her do action songs while I was giving him a gastrostomy feed. When he was 15 months old, and it was apparent that he would need to be tube-fed long term, they had replaced the naso-gastric tube with a more permanent solution, a gastrostomy tube, which is a tube that goes directly through the stomach wall, so that it is less apparent. He still has it all these years later.

Adam had different interests. He would lose himself for hours with a ball of string and all his Bob the Builder toys, demonstrating sheer engineering brilliance by tying Scoop to Muck then weaving the string through the banisters and back down again to tie onto Roly then the string would go around the door handle, under the sofa where I was sitting, back to join Dizzy into this labyrinth, and finally he would show me that pulling the string on one side of the room would make Roly shut the dining room door on the other side of the room. Incredible, particularly since some years later, along with an impressively long list of other conditions, Adam was diagnosed with Dyspraxia. Most crucially, however, it meant he was meaningfully occupied right under my nose for the entire length of time it took to do all Toby's care.

Francesca was 4 and Toby was 3 when Adam came along. His arrival undoubtedly changed our family dynamic for the better. For many different reasons it's very hard to be a single sibling to a severely disabled child, but once there are two siblings the whole family begins to feel less abnormal.

Francesca and Adam have had to put up with a lot of things that no parent would wish for their children. Inevitably, when Toby has been ill and in hospital, they have had a very unfair share of my time. They have seen things that no child should ever have to see, and they have grown up knowing about the life-and-death realities from a very young age, the very realities that most parents do all they can to protect their very young children from witnessing.

I'm a firm believer that children are far more resilient than we give them credit for, and that they can cope with most things, given the right support, as long as they have a solid base, and an unshakeable belief that they are completely, totally, utterly and unconditionally loved, whatever happens.

There have been dozens of ways in which the children have missed out though. Days out and holidays have always been difficult, sometimes impossible. In the early days particularly, Toby had so much medical equipment that going anywhere felt like we first had to pack a medium-sized intensive care unit into the boot of the car. Going any distance meant factoring in stops sometimes every 20 minutes or so to administer Toby's care regime. Try keeping an eye on two small children while doing chest physio on the third in the back seat of a car. Even an occasional trip to the local park felt like an expedition. The other thing is the logistics. Even if you manage to hook everything on the back of a wheelchair - an oxygen cylinder, a feeding pump, a nebuliser and a bag containing drug and syringes, plus changes of clothes for when he is sick, a blanket to put on the ground if he stops breathing and needs CPR, plus goodness only knows what else – how on earth do you also manage to push a wheelchair and a toddler in a buggy?

Money was always tight too. We were always living on either one salary or on benefits. The extra costs of looking after children with disabilities can sky-rocket out of control sometimes. We always had to have the central heating on high, all night as well as all day, because Toby was unable to regulate his own body temperature. He was so often sick, or the gastrostomy feed would spill or leak, or, because he was on a liquid diet, his nappies would leak. Not only did we need twice as many clothes and bedding, we had to have a tumble dryer too, and the washing-machine and tumble dryer were always working at industrial productivity rates. That also meant that both machines would need replacing every year or two simply because they were worn out. Then there were specialist toys or specialist equipment to buy too; once products are marketed to the disability community their price seems to multiply five-fold. Our costs just kept on going up, and I had to learn how to manage money efficiently very quickly.

We did have some highly entertaining times though. On one very warm, summer's day, all my neighbours press-ganged me into taking all three children on a picnic in the park. With five other adults and a whole gang of tiny children, for once there were enough pairs of hands to ensure that all three of my children could be safe and happy, playing in the glorious sunshine. We'd arranged it beforehand, but the manager of the café in the park was very kind in letting me use their electricity sockets for Toby's equipment.

It was an absolutely perfect day and great fun too. We stayed there for hours, well into the evening, with enough food for both lunch and toddler tea in the park, coming home just in time for bathtime.

It was much later, around 10pm, that I had a real shock. I was two syringes short in my gastrostomy supply bag – they must still have been in the children's area of the park.

Back then, gastrostomy feeding was a lot less common than it is today, and the syringes I used were dual purpose and could equally well have been used to inject drugs. I panicked, and visualised the front page of our local paper carrying a story of our local park being used as a drug den by addicts because some poor mother might stumble across one of my missing syringes the following morning.

So in the dead of night, with a couple of neighbours, we returned to the park, armed with torches, and climbed over the fence that surrounds the children's area. We must have studied every single last blade of grass in the entire area, terrified that we may be discovered and have to explain ourselves to a passing policeman.

Two hours later we gave up our search and crept back to our little road, still syringe-less. I held my breath when the local paper came out each Friday for the next few weeks. About 3 months later, collecting the car after a service, the mechanic handed me the two syringes he'd found somewhere deep in the bodywork. To this day, I still don't have a clue how they got there, but at least no one boycotted the park in fear of drug-dealers.

When Adam was a little bit older, he developed into a runner. Not in a fitness-guru, marathon gold-medal kind of a way but in a runner-away way. We'd start walking with me having given him dire warnings about what will happen if he should even think about letting go of the handle of the wheelchair, but something would always catch his eye and he would be off. How do you abandon Toby in the wheelchair and leg it after him? Well you do, but you shouldn't, and what happens to Francesca in the meantime – leave her too or drag her to chase Adam? Crowds were a nightmare; Adam would just weave in and out of people's legs and be gone. It became a regular occurrence to have to get announcements made for people to look out for a small boy who was lost. Every time we were reunited, Adam would be completely bewildered as to why I was worried. "But Mummy, I was never lost, I always knew exactly where I was". This was years before he was diagnosed with ADHD (Attention Deficit Hyperactivity Disorder), I simply couldn't fathom why he had to keep on escaping.

So we had to stop going out. Unless I could get competent care cover for Toby, or an extra pair of hands to help me with all three of them, we simply stayed at home. Even the simplest of family outings like going to the supermarket together were very rare treats for years upon years.

We just had to learn together to make a load of fun at home, which I think we did very successfully most of the time. One thing I did to compensate was that Francesca and Adam's friends always had an open invitation, and most of the time our house was heaving with children. Sleepovers happened most weekends, with Toby taking it all in his stride and loving the company.

Birthdays became enormous celebrations, as did Christmas. All the money other families spend on outings and holidays I'd spend on birthdays to let them know how special they all were. They had the best birthday parties and presents I could possibly afford on a limited income, well thought out gifts that would keep them occupied and engaged for ages, to make all the time they spent at home as much fun as possible.

With a bit of juggling, I did manage to ensure that the two more active children had a lot of after-school activities like Scouts, Brownies, Karate, Swimming, Dancing, Drama, piano and guitar lessons. Around the corner was a Saturday drama school offering dance, drama and singing lessons as a three hour package which made life much easier – no hanging about and waiting with Toby in the back of the car for half an hour hoping he'd stay stable while they were in a 30 minute lesson. I managed to work out some pretty elaborate rota systems with other parents too. If Francesca or Adam wanted to join a particular activity, I would lobby all their friends' parents until we found a friend for them to go with, then we would share the picking up and dropping off. To even try to attempt to do both the taking and the collecting for a short, half hour or an hour-long activity was just never going to happen with Toby around.

When we did venture out as a family, we became experts on where the best disability awareness places were. As the years went by, and Toby's health need emergencies started to recede a little, we became slightly more adventurous. Thorpe Park was less than an hour away and it became our number one place to go. The staff there were always so patient and kind with Toby, and their medical room would always allow us to plug in whatever medical equipment needed electricity. Later, as the other two were diagnosed with disabilities too, it became cost-effective to buy annual passes for each of them. Being disabled, each pass came with an extra carer's ticket, so we were entitled to turn up with six people as many times as we wanted for a whole year for the price of three annual passes. It meant I could bring another adult, and we could also bring a friend of one of the children. The Thorpe Park Annual Pass also entitled us to visit all the other venues in the group too, including Chessington World of Adventures, Alton Towers, Madame Tussauds and the London Eye.

With Toby as part of our family, being able to be up, ready and out early in the morning is virtually impossible, and I would struggle to get him ready and in the car, with all his medical equipment and supplies, and all the way to Thorpe Park by lunchtime. If we had needed to pay their day pass rates each time, we would never have got our money's worth. The best thing about having an annual pass for our family was that this completely took away the time pressure of trying to get there early, or even staying all day once we arrived. We could just go for an hour or so, which we simply could never have afforded to do if we had had to pay the full entrance fee every time.

Butlins became our holiday resort of choice, too. Their staff just bend over backwards to help with Toby, and it was a very safe environment where I could let the other two wander independently a little, too. There is always something to do for everyone, and it really worked well for us. Going abroad was impossible as a family because no one would offer Toby health insurance, but even if that hadn't been a sticking point, I think I'd have been scared stiff about the idea of him getting ill in a foreign country with no access to his rather complex medical notes, and then having to try to explain his condition to doctors who did not speak English well.

As Toby got a little bit older, he was able to access respite facilities on a longer-term basis, sometimes a whole week. However, that still meant we could only get away for 6 days which limited our choices somewhat and certainly we were never able to book a conventional package holiday. I managed a few days in Spain with Francesca and Adam once, and we also managed Euro-Disney for 3 days and a couple of short breaks in Italy. I've just added it up – Francesca, Adam and I spent a total of 21 nights abroad in the full length of Toby's first eighteen years. They both had friends in school who would spend longer than this abroad every single year.

Juggling the needs of three very different children is sometimes a tall order, and it often proved impossible to meet all their needs at the same time.

I always seemed to have several "mummy hats", it often felt that I just couldn't win, and by trying to be the most responsive mother to one of them at any particular moment meant that I was also being completely the wrong type of mother the other two needed.

Little things often make all the difference. I tried as often as possible to do long, chatty bedtimes, complete with a bedtime story, for each of the three children, and I also made sure Francesca, who was the oldest, had a bedtime that was significantly later than Adam's or Toby's, so that she and I could have some "grown-up" time together too. A special treat on a Friday night was to pick a video up from the hire shop on the way home from school, buy some sweets and fizzy drinks, and chill out together on the sofa having quality time together.

It would be lovely to report that all three of my children were always little angels, but no, they could be total horrors at times too. Mostly they played well together, but when they didn't you would have thought that our house was hosting a full-scale guerrilla war. Toby, despite all his butter-wouldn't-melt good looks and desperately ill health, could also be a troublemaker. He was jealous of his little brother once Adam started to walk, and for the next 10 years or so, he would hurl missiles like video tapes or books with laser-precision accuracy in the direction of Adam's head whenever he could. There was one awful moment in a supermarket when Adam was a small baby in a car seat in the body of the shopping trolley, with Toby in the front toddler seat. Toby reached out and picked up a catering-sized glass bottle of tomato ketchup and turned around to drop it on Adam's head. A dad on the other side of the aisle saw what was unfolding and superman-style leapt towards us and caught the bottle just as Toby let go of it. A lot of the time I couldn't leave both the boys in the same room, not easy when we were such a stay-at-home family.

When they were little, we did a lot of playing together, or dressing up, reading stories, doing jigsaws and making music. Francesca loved building dens everywhere – huge sheets draped over the dining-room table became a pirate ship or a cave or a magic island – and the boys loved it when she invited them in too. Toby didn't master crawling until he was four, or walking independently until he was ten, but from fairly early on he could race around the house in what we called "carpet backstroke". The other two would copy him, all of them lying on the floor staring at the ceiling, bending their knees and using their heels to shoot backwards, head first. Despite all my best efforts to keep cushions around the skirting boards, inevitably there were banged heads and outraged tears on a fairly regular basis. Toby was incredibly fast at getting around this way, but with one major drawback, he couldn't turn or reverse when he got to the other end of the room. He became very good at shooting under the furniture and getting himself stuck – I often had to ring a neighbour to come and help me lift a sofa up carefully to find Toby laughing his head off while he was trapped underneath.

This eventually developed into a Toby-orientated version of hide-and-seek, still his favourite ever activity, where everyone we know has to hide in turn according to his very precise rules, a game we still play for hours at least once a week.

In one way or another, every aspect of Francesca and Adam's existence was at least a little bit different from their friends' lives. However, I really don't think it has all been bad. They both have a degree of patience, tolerance, understanding and empathy that is well beyond their years, they both have a strength of character and internal resources and resilience which will set them up for life, and they both have developed enquiring minds and the ability to paint their lives on a broader canvas than many other children manage. Being housebound has enabled them to develop skills that they otherwise may not have done.

One big bugbear moment-of-dread I often had to face was when either Francesca or Adam would come to me and say the words that every parent fears, "I'm bored". We would then sit down together and write a list of 50 or 60 things that they could do to allay the boredom. I thought that was pretty normal, and what every parent did, but once it happened when there were a couple of other mums in the house. They were staring open-mouthed as Francesca and I added more and more activities to the list. Then they started copying the list to use with their kids. So in some ways at least, my kids had very rich lives.

Did the lists help? Of course not. It took me several years to learn that when a child is bored they are going to dig their heels in and be stubbornly and determinedly bored for hours and hours, just because they can. Sometimes boredom is actually over-tiredness, but I also learned never to voice that one, or you get a bored child throwing an angry tantrum as well, protesting vehemently that they aren't tired. If you ever have to cope with a child who is moaning that they are bored, I suggest you buy a Harry Potter Invisibility cloak, either that or lock yourself in the understairs cupboard.

Or you could try the list, here goes, and I hope it works better for you than it ever did for me:

Why don't you do a jigsaw?

What about playing with water?

Would you like to do some drawing?

Or some painting?

Or some colouring in?

What about doing this sticker book?

How about you help me make lunch?

Would you like me to read you a story?

Shall I go and get the dressing up clothes?

What about we get the sheets out so you can build a den?

How about we play with some string?

I know! I've saved all the cardboard boxes for ages – would you like to make something?

What about I push you on the swing in the garden?

Shall I get your bike out of the shed so you can ride it in the garden?

How about we build some bricks?

Would you like to phone Grandad/best friend/next door neighbour?

Shall I get you some ingredients so you can do some food mixing?

What about we make some cakes?

How about I teach you how to sew?

Shall we play hide and seek?

What's on the TV?

Hey, would you like to watch one of your videos?

Wow, look, I've got some chalk – would you like to draw on the garden path?

Hey, please, it'll be fun, and I can teach you how to play hopscotch!

What about you have a bath just so you can play with all the bath toys?

Hey, how about we get the tea-set out and you can make me a nice pretend cup of tea?

Wow, why don't we see if we can do giant footsteps all the way to the front door?

Would you like to play with mummy's make-up?

Shall we paint your nails?

Would you like to paint mummy's nails?

I know, let's phone a friend and see if they can come over?

OK, so that would be boring because there's nothing to do. Shall I see if you can go & play at someone else's house?

How about we make up a story together?

Let's put on some music and dance and sing.

Let's see how high you can count?

Why don't we practice star-jumps?

Why don't we get your skipping rope so you can skip in the garden?

What about we get the saucepans out and make some clatter music?

Let's make up a silly song.

Why don't we record your very own radio show?

Let's play with toy cars.

Have you ever spun around in a circle and see how it feels to get dizzy?

Shall we light a real candle so you can blow it out?

Shall we pretend to be an aeroplane?

Shall we pretend to be a rabbit/horse/spider?

Sort out all the books on the bookcase in alphabetical order.

Would you like to make some Christmas cards (I know it's only July)?

How about we play a board game?

Why don't we tidy your bedroom?

Hey, what would you like Santa Claus to bring you next Christmas? Let's write a list.

(this has now gone on for so long, it feels like Christmas must be next week, but it's still only July).

Hey, let's pretend we're walking on the moon.

Let's sing some silly songs for Toby.

Hey, let's put your your wellies on and see if there are any puddles in the garden to jump in (OK, unlikely in July, but it may just give me 2 minutes peace).

Ooooh, I've got something really special.....I've kept it hidden under the stairs for ages as a surprise, I've got an enormous cardboard box you can sit in, and we can decorate it so it looks like a car!

Hey, why don't I turn on the computer (this was big and risky with a three year old in the late nineties!).

Shall we make some play-dough?

Why don't we dress you up as a pirate, and we can search for buried treasure?

Shall we organise a treasure hunt?

Let's blow some bubbles.

Why don't we get your fuzzy felt out?

Why don't we blow up a load of balloons and see if we can keep them in the air for ages?

Let's get the toy cars out.

Let's get the dolls out.

Let's pretend to be monsters.

Let's practice handstands.

Shall we get some of Toby's syringes and play water pistols?

OK how about we get out the glitter and the glue.

That was always the last resort. If I had to mention glitter I knew I had lost the game. I'm sure the people that live in our old house still haven't managed to clear it all up, or certainly not the bits of it that got wedged behind the skirting board.

Once, during the building of this list, Francesca decided that she would, actually, love to make something with all the cardboard boxes. It kept her occupied for hours, and she created a fabulous object that looked like a television. Big mistake, it was supposed to be a computer. Second big mistake – her total and utter desolation when the darned thing wouldn't switch on!

As the children got a little bit older, other issues developed that needed sensitive handling. For instance, they would sometimes get puzzled when people stared at Toby, so I told them they were staring because not only was Toby absolutely gorgeous, but so were his brother and sister.

Inevitably, once they were at school there was often the odd comment about them having a brother like Toby, but because I always made their friends so welcome, Toby was generally accepted by their whole peer-group. However it wasn't all plain sailing and both Francesca and Adam have endured quite horrific bullying at various times through their school careers.

One of the hardest times was when Toby came out of Guy's Hospital after we had been living there for 8 months. Francesca was only five, and returned to a school that she had only spent a few weeks at before she had had to transfer to the hospital school. Guy's is a very prestigious leading Central London teaching hospital, where some very sick children are cared for and treated at the cutting edge of medical technology. Inevitably, some of these children don't make it.

While we were there we had lived alongside a number of different families, sharing the load with each other and becoming very close friends very quickly. Several of these families never got to take their children home.

So Francesca, returning to a mainstream Reception Class where all the other little girls are playing mummies and daddies, doing pop-song dance routines in the playground and swapping Barbie clothes, was a fish completely out of water. Unless children live in a warzone, it's very rare for a child to witness so many deaths at such close quarters, so her experiences were virtually unique. Her peer-group at school were only four and five years old. There was no one else who could even envisage the awful things she had witnessed. Children gravitate towards each other often based on shared experiences or common ground and they shun anyone who doesn't fit it. Francesca was a world apart in terms of recent experiences, and she found it very difficult to settle and fit in.

She was clearly very unhappy at school and not making friends easily. She had also spent two terms at the Guy's Evelina Hospital School where the classes were so tiny that she got individual attention, and being naturally very bright, she was also streets ahead of her classmates academically, and on top of everything else, she wasn't being stretched in class.

I had umpteen discussions with the school staff, who all denied that there was anything wrong. Eventually the head teacher told me that the only thing wrong with Francesca was that she was unloved and uncared for, because I was far to busy with Toby to give her the time and attention she needed. So the blame for everything was firmly laid at my door – it was all my fault.

You have to watch out for this – parents with families like ours make very easy scapegoats. Anything at all that goes even a tiny bit pear-shaped at school and teachers will point the finger of blame at us time and time again. It's so easy for other people to make assumptions and come to the conclusion that the healthy siblings must be being neglected. I know in my heart that that was never, ever the case. In fact, looking back, I am convinced that I worked so hard back-pedalling to ensure that Francesca and Adam never felt left out, that I probably over-compensated, and they ended up with more, not less, parental input as a result.

One recurrent and very real fear that faces parents like us is what happens to our disabled child in the future when we can no longer care for them. The sheer terror of what Toby's future may bring never goes away, and is capable of waking me up in the middle of the night in a cold sweat. There are so many stories of abuse towards vulnerable adults that his future has always simply scared me stiff with worry.

Being Toby's brother or sister is a life-long relationship, but I simply never thought it was fair to burden Francesca and Adam with a binding expectation that they will one day take on that responsibility. It will one day be their choice, and I hope they both know I trust their judgement and integrity so that, if they choose not to take on that responsibility, they will have valid reasons for making that choice.

I have made provision for Toby's future, and I have nominated close family friends to share the decision-making on Toby's behalf. I have also left written instructions that, if Francesca or Adam feel they want to take on some level of responsibility for Toby, they can opt into this small "Toby Team" once they have reached the age of 25. If they choose not to take on that responsibility I hope they are able to step away completely guilt and blame-free. I want them both to know that they have one short life each, and however they choose to spend it, they do so with my blessing.

TIPS, TRICKS AND STRATEGIES

Your other children, from the very start, will be learning so much about compassion, empathy and consideration. Praise them every time you see them doing something kind for their less able sibling.

Find ways to have fun at home, let them develop their imagination and don't get too stressed about the messes they make.

I got rid of carpets in favour of laminate flooring. It's so much easier to clear up vomit, leaked gastrostomy feeds, messy play and spillages.

Encourage their friends to play at your house. It is so important that their peer-group get to know their disabled sibling too. The more other children understand and are able to accept, the less likelihood of bullying or being picked on.

Try to spend a couple of minutes getting them involved with an activity before attending to your child with disabilities, because otherwise it may be ages before you can touch base again, and meanwhile your more able children may be getting bored and fractious.

If they are small, find fun ways to include them while you are caring for their sibling, so you can supervise them too.

Investigate value days out and find a way of making them happen, including concessionary rates or annual passes. It made a huge difference to our family once I was able to buy each child an annual pass for Thorpe Park, and it meant that we were able to bring an extra adult each time at no extra cost, making the whole outing much more doable.

Focus on fun. No matter how tough things are, it will lighten your mood and make things easier to deal with. Fun is contagious, and it's also essential for children to have loads of it.

Find every way you can to let all your children know how loved and how special they are.

If school gets tricky for your child, the school may blame you and your home situation. The more you protest or argue your case, the more they assume it must be your fault. I never found the right answer, but I found plenty of wrong ones, the worst being that I let myself get so upset and hurt by it. If I had my time again I would just rise above it emotionally, because that level of ignorance isn't worth ruining your day over.

CHAPTER 8
Becoming the Expert

Slowly but surely, you become your child's expert. If I had started medical school on the day that Toby was born, I would have worked my way up to Consultant level at least by now. In fact, if you take into account that I've been studying my kids twenty-four hours a day, seven days a week, without even holiday or sickness absence, I have worked many more hours than doctors do throughout their careers, so I should be well into retirement by now.

Without the paper qualification, it can be difficult to be taken seriously by many professionals. Some of them, particularly in the medical profession, can seem threatened by our knowledge and confidence, and it is sometimes very hard to stand your ground and ensure that you are listened to, which can add to the frustrations of parenting children like ours.

As well as doctors, you'll be dealing with all sorts of other professionals, and there will also be meetings galore to attend. These are all supposedly about your child, but there will be all sorts of other issues being played out around the table competing for importance. The biggest of these is always budgets, which means every meeting will carry an unspoken conflict of interests. Your role is to get the best treatment, care, education and services for your child. Their job is to protect their budgets, and some of the people you come in contact with will be so defensively protective of spending any money that you would honestly believe that it was coming out of their own family purse, to the extent that they act as if it's a straight choice between feeding their own children or giving your child what they so desperately need.

In most of the around the table meetings I've attended, there have been upwards of eight people, each representing different departments or organisations. Sometimes I've attended 8 or 10 of these meetings in a year, often with virtually the same group of people sitting around the table. It's not unusual for the meetings to last

90 minutes or so. If you start adding up people's salaries, then calculating their hourly rates, their travel time and expenses, the room hire rate, the time it's taken them to write their beloved reports before the meeting and to plan for the meeting itself, checking the minutes of the meetings afterwards as well as reporting back to their managers, however much is each of these meetings actually costing the tax-payer? There have been many meetings I've attended when the salary cost of meeting attendance plus all these other add-ons must easily exceed £1,000.

So they are spending enormous sums of money in order to tell parents that they don't have the money to spend on the very children that these services have been designed to support. It's a dichotomy that these people just don't even notice, and it would be almost funny if it weren't so sad.

There is another aspect to all of this too. Very few professionals are able or willing to take a decision alone, nor are they able to make any cost-dependent decisions around the table during the meeting that parents are invited to attend. Instead, the sort of care our children receive is increasingly dependent on a decision by committee, with no one having the confidence or autonomy to make a unilateral decision, and no parents present to see how decisions are reached.

Whenever a group of people make a collective decision, compromises happen, nuances get sidelined, any decisions taken often become watered-down versions of what is really needed, and therefore tend to be much less effective.

So even if, at one of these countless meetings you will be required to attend, it is decided that something may need to be changed that will require funding of some sort, the best you can expect to come out of the meeting with is a decision to take it "to panel". Panels are held within social services departments behind closed doors, normally with the names of the people who sit on these panels being kept a closely guarded secret. They meet regularly, perhaps once or twice a month, and decide on a case-by-case basis, which child or family will be awarded funding for extra services and which won't.

I have a fantasy vision of what these meetings must actually be like. I imagine them to be held in a Henry VIII style court, with the participants wearing bright red, fur trimmed robes, and the Chair of the meeting wearing a bejewelled crown as well. The whole scene is sort of crossed with an Alice in Wonderland feeling about it too, and one by one, a courtier approaches and pleads for the family in their care. At random, the Chair-King barks his or her arbitrary judgement, a mix of "Granted" "No Chance, who do they think they are" "Maybe" and of course an occasional "Off with their heads".

OK, so we're in the 21st century, and it's highly improbable that it's carried on like that, but if you were at the mercy of some of the strange decisions that come out of that meeting you'd see that it might as well be.

Back to the meeting that we actually get invited – or should I say summoned? - to attend. As well as that big funding elephant in the room, there will be a number of other things going on that we can only begin to guess at; no matter how good we are at reading between the lines. Things like protecting their own or their organisation's reputation, political alliances being formed, petty old scores to be settled – all sorts of undercurrents happening around you while they pretend it's all about your child.

Throughout Toby's childhood, there were two recurrent big issues that were discussed time and time again; his behaviour and his nutrition. Toby, although delightfully affable the vast majority of the time, could throw temper tantrums that over the years developed into quite frightening and aggressive behaviour at times. He wasn't diagnosed with Autism until he was nearly 18, so I didn't know that what I was dealing with were meltdowns rather than tantrums. The behaviour was a very big issue, particularly as he grew bigger and stronger into his teens, and he would occasionally also go on destructive rampages through the house breaking things at quite an alarming speed.

Feeding too was an enormous issue. When he was about twelve some tests on his throat determined that it might, at some point in the future, be possible to wean him off the gastrostomy and introduce solid food instead. It was a really exciting moment; we were given the go-ahead to tentatively try him on proper food through his mouth. However, we were warned that, since he had never eaten, he might be fearful about it, and that the best way to move forward would be to let him guide us at his own pace, introducing food slowly and only if he showed enthusiasm. Even with this big breakthrough, he was incapable of chewing, his swallow mechanism was still very rudimentary so he would run a very high risk of choking and so therefore would need careful monitoring and supervision, but we were still given the green light to try.

I was delighted, overjoyed, it was everything I had ever wanted to hear, and I envisaged having loads of fun with him as he tried a whole variety of different tastes and textures over the coming weeks and months. I passed on this news to all the different settings he spent time with - school, after-school clubs, respite, carers - but cautioned extreme care and to take it entirely at his pace.

Disappointingly, among many of the professionals, It became like some sort of competition. Every meeting a representative from each of these organisations would wax lyrical, each trying to out-do the others in proving how much Toby enjoyed eating, and how many new foodstuffs they had managed to get him to try. Meanwhile at home, he doggedly refused all efforts at getting him to eat. He would shout in protest, keeping his mouth firmly closed, sometimes even wrestling the plate from me and angrily throwing it against the wall. He was making it loud and clear that he was not willing to try proper eating for me, he was absolutely adamant that gastrostomy feeding was his only choice at home.

So we started a period that lasted several years where apparently he was eating fantastically well everywhere else, but refused normal eating at home. Yet he was losing weight, so how much was he really eating at all these other institutions? I knew anecdotally, from talking to junior front-line care staff, that he sometimes struggled to eat, and that sometimes he wouldn't eat at all, and even more worryingly, that there were occasional choking episodes too.

Yet all I was hearing in meetings was that his eating was going marvellously well everywhere else, and it was only me that was failing dismally.

It's generally the managers of these organisations who attend these meetings. They are very aware that their funding often depends on their reputation, so they won't readily want to admit that they and their staff are anything other than completely in charge and on top of each and every situation. Additionally, if a child chokes whilst on site at a school or childcare provider, there are long forms to fill out, investigations, and care staff know that they are likely to be in the spotlight of possible cause and effect. The upshot is that there are times when these incidents simply don't get formally reported and recorded, because to do so is to open a whole can-of-worms of investigations to look at for possible negligence, which could, in turn, damage their reputation, which could perhaps halt their funding.

It was exactly the same story with his temper tantrums/meltdowns. They simply never happened anywhere else apparently. I knew full-well they did, because care staff had told me about incidents on numerous occasions, but they obviously never got recorded for similar reasons. So officially, they didn't have any behavioural problems at all with Toby.

It's very difficult to challenge these issues in a big meeting where there can be 3 or 4 representatives from organisations all swearing blind that he eats perfectly and is always impeccably behaved. Maybe these managers simply believed their own myths, it may well be that they too were kept in the dark by junior care staff who wanted to avoid being in trouble, but I somehow always doubted it.

What happens? I go into these meetings and tell it exactly like it is, that he has aggressive meltdowns that I'm unable to contain or handle anymore, and that he refuses to eat. Around the table, everyone is openly sympathetic, but it clearly becomes an issue to do with his home-life somehow, because that's the only place it's officially happening.

It's difficult to state categorically that I've been told that these things happen by junior members of their staff, because I simply don't want to sour relationships with the people who care for Toby by dropping them in it.

So a new myth develops. It must be my fault. Maybe Toby and I don't have a good relationship. Infuriating.

Sometimes, before a meeting, I would actually ring one of the people who would be attending and quietly let them know that I was aware things weren't always great regarding the eating and aggression issues when he was in their care, and sometimes I would get an acknowledgement that they knew this, and a promise that they would spill the beans and tell the truth in the next meeting. Sometimes they did, most times they didn't, but even when they did, the issues would be described in such vague, watered-down terms that it barely registered with the other attendees. I've often wondered why. Perhaps there is sometimes an element of them feeling protective towards Toby himself, and maybe they don't want to paint too negative a picture of a young lad who, despite the occasional aggressive outburst, is overwhelmingly endearing and lovable.

However, protecting their own interests, their budgets and their reputations often seems more important than establishing the truth about the support that Toby genuinely needs and deserves. One day he will leave home, and unless it has been acknowledged that he exhibits challenging behaviour across all settings, and that he struggles with eating and has the occasional choking episode, he will not be placed in the right environment with staff fully informed and able to cope with his needs, nor will he qualify for the safest level of one-to-one care that he so obviously needs.

Instead, the inference is that it is all my fault, rather than a conspiracy of silence. This becomes a big issue too, because assumptions start being made that I may have poor parenting skills. Perhaps I am not responding effectively to his needs, or that he and I have a hostile relationship, or a hundred and one other things that could, potentially, lead to a situation where they felt I wasn't competent to care for him anymore. Fortunately, budget considerations work in the parents' favour here – it's cheaper to leave our children in our care at home than to take them away.

The other obvious factor that they never quite took on board was that, when Toby was at school or at a childcare organisation, they had a very generous staff to child ratio, and the staff were only responsible for looking after the children in their care throughout their standard working hours. At home, I was on my own with three children, with no backup or help if things got out of hand, I also had meals to cook, a house to run, and a dozen other things to try and achieve at the same time. Yet I always felt my competence was judged as if all things were equal on a like-for-like basis.

So what did I do? I often felt I was in a very difficult situation. By stating the full truth of how I was struggling with his behaviour and eating issues, I might also be creating an impression that I was not coping, but to pretend that everything was hunky-dory was not a viable option either. It often felt that I was stuck between a rock and a hard place.

It's very hard to spell out the severity of all the incidents we were facing at home when I've just heard everyone around the table stating, one by one, that he was a paragon of virtue everywhere else, and it felt that I was going against the grain to be negative about my own son in these meetings. I felt under a subtle, but very real, pressure to join in and minimise the real problems, but I also knew that to do so was not going to do Toby any favours whatsoever in the long term. It was hard, but I tried to tell things as they really were at home. By doing so, I was continually swimming against the tide, and I'm sure the professionals would have been much happier if I hadn't been so open.

It's a fine line to tiptoe along, telling the truth but in such a way that doesn't damage your own credibility or reduce the goodwill around the table. To be honest, there always was a lot of goodwill extended towards our family by the professionals, certainly by the time he reached his teenage years. I had known many of them for several years, and they knew me well and I had excellent, relaxed relationships with most of them.

However, the balance of power is always in their hands. If you try to challenge these people while they are sitting around the table, it just won't work. If you then tell a social worker what's actually happening, they either find it hard to believe or they kindly tell you that all these people are trying to spare your feelings, and don't want to be openly critical about your child when others are present. Sometimes all I really needed was a nice, solid brick wall to bang my head against.

What I have described is typical of an overall agenda to minimise your child's degree of disability and need. It happens over and over again, and can be difficult, if not impossible, to counter. Factor in as well how these meetings are run, one of you against all of them. It can be very intimidating, and very difficult to be heard properly if you feel they are ganging up on you. They gang up very politely, and use a lot of different tactics to undermine you, and it can be very hard indeed.

I sometimes dream of turning the tables on them. Having each one of them walk in alone to a group of Special Parents and see how they cope. We could each go around the table and put them on the spot by asking them individually about each of our children. That's another issue, too. There is an unspoken rule that you aren't supposed to talk about your child's care package to other parents. One of the ways they make many people conform is to make them feel guilty for receiving so much funding, that they are embarrassed to talk to other parents openly in case they are accused of taking more than their fair share from the funding pot. How clever is that! They are masters at divide and rule. Individually, they expect us to walk into these meetings like a Dickensian embodiment of Victorian poverty, and beg for a crust or two for our children, with a lot of cap-doffing and reverence along the way.

Never, in all my years of attending meetings, have I met any of these professionals who have a child of their own with disabilities. So they really don't have an inkling of what it is really like, full-on, 24/7 to cope with the relentless, non-stop needs of our children. Yet these are the people who are charged with passing judgements on how well or otherwise we are coping, who are very quick to jump to conclusions, and, because they have a job where they are paid to sit in long meetings with parents like me, they actually believe that they really do know how it is.

Before the meeting there is a lot you can do to prepare. You are likely to receive an invitation list as well as an agenda. Be very clear in your own mind what the big issues are at the moment, and what you ideally want to achieve from the meeting. However, if there are several big issues, choose the three biggest ones, any more than that will give them plenty of scope for wriggling out of doing anything, or doing one tiny thing on a relatively minor issue that really doesn't count for much.

It helps if you can get to grips with the current buzzwords and phrases being used by the Social Services fraternity, so that you, too, can speak their language, even though it sometimes sounds absurd. There may be a newly introduced sociological ideology that that everyone around the table has signed up to with unwavering devotion and single-minded belief. I've had some really hilarious times with other special needs parents when we try to include as many of their phrases into our conversations as possible. Our children become "service users", going out and about becomes "accessing the community", being cross about how our children's needs are consistently sidelined and ignored becomes "learning to manage our own expectations". Sometimes it's only a sense of humour that keeps us sane.

There will be members of the multi-disciplinary team that you trust more than others, and feel are more on your side. If these people have been omitted from the invitation list, you can ask for them to be included, and if for any reason that doesn't happen, you can then ask them to write a report for you to take with you.

If it was a particularly key meeting with a lot at stake, I would sometimes ring a few of the invited professionals a few days beforehand. It's helpful to know whether the ones you really like and trust are able to attend or not. If they can't attend, sometimes I've asked them if they would have time to write a report to submit instead. There may well be things you really would like to see on that report, and if that's been the case with me, I have asked them, very directly, to raise these certain points, offering to send them an email clearly stating the key points that would help. Many times, a few days later, I've had to suppress a smile when I've been handed a copy of the report once the meeting is underway, and realised that the lovely professional concerned has copied and pasted sections from my email and inserted them into the main section of their report. If you can get them on your side, some of these professionals really will go the extra mile for you, even virtually allowing you to write the report on your child stating exactly what needs to be said.

If they are able to attend, even better. It's much easier to gain their support in a meeting if you've had a friendly, chatty discussion about your concerns in the few days beforehand.

Look at the previous meeting's minutes, and ensure you have completed all the action points that were assigned to you, or that you at least go into the meeting with solid reasons as to why they haven't yet been achieved.

Network with other local parents, find out what you can about their recent meetings. Are there trends, such as is everyone having their Direct Payment hours cut by 20%? Is there anyone in your network who actually reversed the trend and got it increased? What factors made this happen? If there is anyone attending who you haven't met before, are there other parents who know them? What are they like? What services are other children currently being offered?

You learn far far more from other parents than anyone else. If parents don't tell you about things like play-schemes, respite facilities or new therapies on offer locally, you won't know what's on offer. This sort of information isn't always freely available any other way. They don't exactly advertise good, new services because then everyone would want them and with funding and budgets dominating nearly every decision that's made, that would simply never do.

I wasn't always as good at preparing for meetings as I am now. I used to hate ringing professionals beforehand and asking favours. Over time, though, I realised that the professionals were often having pre-meeting chats with little deals being made or agendas being planned privately. Deals and agendas that often have absolutely nothing to do with your child. Eventually I learnt how to do it too, but with a difference; I only ever did it to protect the interests of the children, who were supposed to be the central theme of these meetings anyway.

Have there been any recent incidents concerning your child at other settings that may back up your arguments? Have you kept a note of the date, or the person you spoke to about it? Keep records of anything like this because you never know when it might help.

Special school head teachers, school nurses and class teachers can all be very useful allies in Social Services meetings. Talk to them beforehand, sound them out about the issues that are concerning you, and even ask them to attend if you think they will help. Head teachers are particularly well-regarded in the hierarchical food-chain, and I've been lucky enough to have had some really supportive ones walking into meetings with me.

Local Authorities are subject to a legal framework which underpins their duty and obligations to our children. This legal framework is subject to change from time to time, with new Acts being passed or the current ones amended. Additionally, each Local Authority sometimes interprets the law slightly differently, and with no two children with disabilities being in exactly identical situations, there is a lot of scope for a great degree of variance in how it is applied, even within the same local authority.

It really helps if you can do your homework regarding your child's legal position. There are a number of websites that make this quite easy to do, and there are a lot of parents who can share this sort of information.

Sometimes, it can boil down to using the right words that can open the appropriate access to funding. For example, if you talk about a sibling who is finding her disabled brother difficult to deal with because they sometimes fight, you may be told that there are no current services to support siblings. However, if you say the same thing in different words, for example, that you have concerns that your small daughter is at a high risk of serious injury caused by the meltdown-induced aggressive behaviour of her older brother, you may successfully achieve your objective in getting more Direct Payment hours agreed.

After the meeting, you will get the minutes eventually. However, sometimes they don't seem to bear much relation to the meeting as you remember it. That's why having someone taking notes is so important, and don't be afraid to challenge the minutes, putting in writing that you would like them to be altered to better reflect what was said, being very specific about which points need to be altered.

Despite doing everything you possibly can to prepare, sometimes it can feel like you are talking into thin air, being marginalised, and you're getting nowhere and not being listened to properly.

One philosophy that I have developed and adhere to whatever happens is that I never complain. Ever. About anything at all.

I learned my lesson on that one in the early days when Toby and I were together in hospital while he was desperately ill. A nurse did something to him that caused him to deteriorate very fast and he nearly died. I was furious so I put in a formal complaint. What happened next was simply awful. The entire staff simply sent me to Coventry and refused to talk to me. I was a young mother of a seriously ill child, who was also caring for her toddler at the bedside 12 hours a day, and I was totally reliant on these staff, who were the only people I saw for hours at a time. I needed them to stay with Toby while I went off to the loo or to change Francesca's nappy or find some food for her.

At a stroke, all of that friendship and support was withdrawn, and to this day I still don't have the words to describe how isolated, desolate, frightened and lost that made me feel.

Filing a complaint to a statutory body is a big number. It's not like walking into a shop and complaining about their service because the checkout person was unfriendly, and they sort it out there and then, apologise, give you a money-off coupon, and it's done and dusted. Oh no, complaining to a hospital or similar establishment means kick-starting a chain of events that may lead to the public humiliation and scapegoating of members of staff or their managers, with a myriad of forms, meetings and all sorts of who knows what else on the way. So the staff hate it, quite rightly, because it is such a ridiculously cumbersome process. Unfortunately they all too often take their dislike out on the messenger, many time a parent, the person who blew the whistle and complained in the first place.

There has been a lot in the press in recent years about how appallingly whistleblowers are treated in the NHS, and I can so see what happens. However, when you are in my situation, with a child who is totally reliant on these organisations for everything and your child is likely to be an inpatient time and time and time again, it simply isn't an option to complain, because you so badly need the goodwill of the whole hospital team.

Instead, I very gently point out errors in the most tactful and diplomatic of ways. If that doesn't work and I am seriously worried about Toby's safety, I simply ensure I never leave his bedside for more than a moment or two at a time, and try to enlist trusted family members or good friends to help me support Toby on the ward.

Social Services and Education aren't quite as bad as the NHS in handling complaints, but it's still not something I'd want to do very often. Some parents I know have gone to see their MP, or have even engaged the services of a specialist disability lawyer. A letter from somebody influential like this can work wonders. However, most of us can't afford to hire good lawyers, and we often don't have the time either to visit our MP. If you do go down this route, I would suggest that you don't overuse these options because you will lose goodwill if you do. However, it's quite disturbing how decisions that you have been completely unable to reverse are swiftly changed after they receive a letter from either an MP or a solicitor on your child's behalf.

Generally, though, it's important to remember that you are likely to be working with these people for a very long time. Building up good relationships based on trust and integrity will pay you dividends over and over again, although it's not always easy to establish and maintain this level of support and rapport.

It isn't always possible, but it can help if you can get some of the meetings combined. Occasionally I managed to combine a care-plan meeting with a school annual review meeting. Each of these meetings will take a full half day out of your week, plus all the planning and preparation time, and the recovery calming-down time afterwards, so if you can manage to kill two birds with one stone every now and again it really does help.

It's rare to get the medical profession to engage with other agencies at these meetings; in all the meetings I attended, despite being invited to virtually every single one, we have never had a representative from our GP practice attend. This may change with the new legislation that is being introduced, which combines the health, social care and education needs of a child with disabilities all in the one document, but I wouldn't be too hopeful.

Quite frankly, these meetings can be appalling, and can completely destroy your confidence and self-esteem in the process. It is quite awful to have to walk into a room, knowing that you will be expected to lay bare every aspect of your family life to people that you may well not trust at all, who will then record all this information and be free to share it with whoever they deem fit to share it with. The level of intrusiveness is shocking, and the way it can make you feel very vulnerable and exposed is just not fair. Meanwhile, you can often see that the other salaried participants have no way of fully understanding just how difficult your home-life can be because they have no hands-on benchmark to measure it against, and yet they can, and they do, judge you quite openly, often suggesting "better" ways you could do things at home.

Over the years, I've had no option but to take a different attitude about these meetings, both for the sake of my own sanity, and to prevent me from accidentally leaning across a desk and strangling one or two of them.

So I have reached a point where I almost actually enjoy them. I know the score as well as the point-scoring undercurrents, and I just so love it when I play them at their own game and aim to win, or at worst to draw even. It's always better to get even than to be angry.

It took me years, but I now handle these meetings much better than I used to. Here are my suggestions.

TIPS, TRICKS AND STRATEGIES

Always get there early, so you're not backfooted by conversions having started before your arrival.

Make small-talk. Chat, laugh and be charmingly pleasant to all and sundry before the meeting begins.

Always take someone with you to every meeting if you can.

Both of you dress as smartly as possible. It's much easier to be intimidated if you look like you've been dragged through a hedge backwards and they are all suited and booted with perfectly applied make-up.

Get your "someone" to take notes, or at least look as if they are taking copious notes. An A4 lined pad in a clipboard folder doesn't cost much, but it creates a very professional image, and they are always a little intimidated by notes being taken of what is actually said.

Most of these meetings start by going around the table introducing themselves one by one. When it's your turn, have a lovely photo of your child on your phone, and pass it around to show everyone. It's the sort of thing proud parents do all the time, but by doing it now, you are also gently reminding everyone exactly who this meeting is supposed to be about.

Your voice is the one voice in the room that is unequivocally on your child's side, and the more it is heard, the more your child is remembered.

Whenever you get a group of professionals together in a room, they just can't help it, but they often speak what can seem like another language. If they start talking in jargon, or use initials as acronyms instead of saying whatever it is in full, just interrupt as nicely as possible and politely ask what that means. I suspect that sometimes certain professionals do actually do it deliberately as a way to marginalise, intimidate and exclude you, which they have absolutely no right whatsoever to do. I used to find it hard to admit that I didn't understand something, as if that was in some way confirming their belief that I was in some way less intelligent than they were, but once I started doing it I started really enjoying myself. It stops them in mid-flow, it spotlights to the others that they may have been intending to undermine you, which will cause them embarrassment, and it gives your voice an extra chance to be heard.

Stay as cool, calm and collected as possible. Showing emotions in these meetings is often playing directly into their hands. Do whatever it takes to try not to cry and not to get angry. It gives them too easy an excuse to diminish everything else you say in the meeting as being feeling rather than fact led, and they already have enough tactics to undermine you, try not to make it even easier for them.

Adopt a professional attitude. These people are at work, and therefore they come into these meetings with a "work-mode" mentality. If you can try get onto the same wavelength by taking a more objective approach, you will be able to build better rapport around the table, and therefore, ultimately, achieve more for your child.

Use vocabulary that will resonate with them, either by mirroring or repeating their phraseology, or determining to use factual-based wording rather than feeling-based wording. Sentences like "I am concerned about my son's overall calorfic intake" are much more effective than "I'm worried that he isn't eating enough". It shouldn't be, but it is. Basically try and talk like one of them.

Remember they are all being paid for being here, you are not. They are not called "Public Servants" for nothing. You are the public; they are supposed to be serving you, not back-footing you or undermining you.

The budgets and funding streams that they hold the keys to are paid for by the public purse specifically for the purpose of helping children like ours. Funding is their job, your child is priceless, so don't let them intimidate you by talking about budget cuts or reductions in funding. They have a statutory duty to provide the services your child needs, how they pay for it is their problem, not yours.

Sometimes you may get overwhelmed. Too many people are saying too many things too quickly and your brain needs a bit longer to process things. Sometimes right in the middle of feeling like this, someone asks you a question. Don't be afraid or ashamed to ask them to say things again, or to admit that you're still focused on the point someone made a few minutes ago. They do these meetings day in and day out, we don't. They are not emotionally involved with the things being discussed, we are. I've sometimes had to admit that I haven't taken anything on board whatsoever for several minutes because I'm still trying to understand what was being said earlier. True professionals understand this, and they will generally be very understanding and helpful, and be happy to recap. It's better to be honest, than to plough along with the meeting when your mind is elsewhere.

Every now and again, particularly if something helpful or even unpleasant has been said, ask if these points are all being minuted.

Don't volunteer to do too much. Sometimes minutes have been produced and nearly all the "Action Points" are things for me to do.

Ask when the minutes will be produced. Sometimes I have only received the minutes a day or two before the follow-up meeting is scheduled.

CHAPTER 9
Being in Hospital

For many of our children, hospitals are likely to become a very large part of family life on and off over the next several years, both as an inpatient and as an outpatient. You will get to know your local hospital far better than you would ever wish to, and there may well be other hospitals with specialist units where you and your child will also spend a considerable amount of time. In total, my children have helped me acquire an intimate knowledge of the workings, the layout and the environs of over ten different hospitals during the last few years, with long in-patient stays in each one.

Whenever your child is admitted to hospital, you're probably exhausted already, not just because you will have just spent several hours in the Accident and Emergency Department, but because you may have also spent the previous few days with a very ill, rapidly deteriorating child, doing everything you know how to do to prevent another hospital admission. Consequently, you may well already be sleep-deprived and just about finished.

Now though, you are in a strange environment, and it may be sinking in that your child is seriously ill, so that's adding to your stress levels too. You are most likely to be overwhelmed with fear, worry and panic. Everything seems to happen so fast, there is too much to assimilate, and all you can manage is to cope with each minute as it happens, one at a time.

Resident Parents in Hospital

First of all, you need to make a difficult decision; is there any way at all you can stay overnight, every night with your child? I can't emphasise strongly enough how important it is to stay as a resident parent if you possibly can. If you have more than one child, and no partner or close family and friends who you can easily call on, wrack your brains and think if there is anyone you know who you could trust to ask them to look after your other children overnight. Or if you can't stay, could somebody else stay on the ward instead; maybe a grandparent or other close relative?

Toby has never been left alone in hospital overnight. Mostly I've stayed with him, but my father, my sister and Toby's Dad have also stayed on many occasions to share the load. I'm so glad he has never been on his own. There just aren't enough staff on the ward to properly care for your child, certainly no one with time to give long, comforting cuddles in the middle of the night to a frightened child who may also be in pain. Accidents and mistakes can and do happen on hospital wards. I could write a whole extra book just documenting some of the near-misses Toby himself has had whilst in hospital. There have been some really frightening errors made by staff even with our family at his bedside keeping a watchful eye. I dread to think what might have happened if he hadn't always had a close family member there to support him.

Even on a children's ward, staff are not always experts with disabled or special needs children. They don't necessarily have someone who would be able to understand your child's way of communication, and even if they do, chances are that person can't always be available whenever your child needs to communicate something important to them. I was on a ward once where there was a non-verbal little boy, whose parents had been called away to a meeting. He was getting very agitated, and although staff were walking over to him every 10-15 minutes, they weren't engaging with him, and he was becoming progressively more distressed. I walked over to his bed, and immediately realised that he was trying to tell the nursing staff that he badly needed a drink, using sign language. In the previous 90 minutes or so, some 5 or 6 members of staff had seen him make exactly the same sign, but because they didn't understand even the very basic signs, he had been left thirsty.

Sometimes, frightened, disorientated children will wander if they are left on their own. And children, especially those with learning disabilities or autism, will not understand the importance of intravenous drips, and may pull the cannula out of their arm. Toby is highly skilled at doing that.

Staff may not have the time to feed your child or coax them into eating or drinking in the way that you or a close friend can do.

Doctors may make decisions on your child's care while you are not at the bedside. Your input in any decision is often invaluable since you are the expert on your child. Sometimes decisions taken may not be the best ones, and you may be the only one who remembers that the same decision didn't work during a previous admission. You will want to be in the driving seat and you need to be party to any treatment options or decisions made about your child's care.

If you really can't stay on the ward with your child, there are compromises. Maybe it is possible that you could stay until your child is asleep and settled for the night. Perhaps you can ask the staff to ring you, even in the dead of night, if your child's condition deteriorates in any way. I would suggest you write a list about your child's likes, dislikes, habits and communication methods, and hand it to the nurses. If possible, also leave a copy by the bedside. Maybe there is another parent on the ward close-by who would be happy to keep an eye on your child too? If that's the case, the ward probably has strict rules that one parent isn't allowed to pick up someone else's child, so the support they can offer is likely to be limited.

If you're able to stay, there are two things you need to get sorted next. First, it helps to know how the land lies in terms of the practicalities, and second, you are going to need a support network like you've never needed one before.

The Practicalities

Your child needs you more than ever right now, so it's incredibly important that you don't get ill too, and that you find a way to manage these new pressures for however long your child will be an inpatient. Toby's longest stay was 8 months, his shortest was 3 weeks. Although the vast majority of children are in and out of hospital within a day or so, children like ours can be much more complex, and their hospital stays are often considerably longer. So, hopefully, your child won't be kept in for too long, but even the shortest stays are a huge shock to the system for you, and looking after yourself and finding a way to cope with this new situation is of paramount importance.

We can come back to the stresses you're likely to be under, but for now, let's look at the basics, the information you are going to need to keep yourself from going under.

If I was asked what is the single most important thing to have with you when you are in hospital, without a doubt I would say **DON'T FORGET YOUR MOBILE PHONE CHARGER.** Keeping in contact with friends and family is essential, and if you forget absolutely everything else, as long as you have a working phone you can ask someone to bring them in!

Parking

It may seem trivial, but hospital car parks charge the earth these days, and if your car is still parked in the hospital car park and you forget it and leave it there for several days, you may need a bank loan to drive it away! Also, you will be very reliant on visitors, so anything you can find out about cheaper ways to park right now, the better. Here are some questions to ask, either of the ward staff, or ask other parents on the ward.

> ***How much are the car-park charges?***
>
> ***Do parents of in-patient children qualify for free or discounted parking?***
>
> ***If so, how do I organise a parking permit?***
>
> ***Is the car-park big enough for the busy times like visiting hours?***
>
> ***What nearby side-street parking is there, and how easy is it to find a space?***

If you have a Blue Badge, where are the disabled parking bays?

Are Blue Badge holders allowed to park in staff-designated parking bays?

Public Transport

Again, you may need this information for visitors

What bus routes go past the hospital and how often?

How late do they run and how early do they start?

Are there any buses that actually drive into the hospital grounds?

What about trains, the Tube or trams?

Where can you get a coffee?

Sometimes, children's wards have a "Parent's Room" where parents can make themselves a cup of tea or coffee, often with a fridge and a toaster too.

Is there a parent's kitchen on the ward? It's also important to know whether tea/coffee/milk/sugar/bread etc is provided by the ward or if it needs to be brought in by parents.

Where is the hospital restaurant?

What are it's opening hours?

Does it have a vending machine you can use out-of-hours to get drinks or snacks?

Do parents of inpatient children qualify for reduced-cost meals?

Does the hospital restaurant provide take-away containers so I can eat beside my child's bed?

Am I allowed to eat on the ward?

Some hospitals also have volunteer-run little teashops, serving drinks, cakes and snacks, often at a fraction of the price of the main hospital canteen. They may have restricted opening hours and a little bit of a quirky feel about them, but they can be an oasis of calm away from the chaos and cacophony of confused thoughts badgering your brain for attention. These little teashops are often run by very kind grandmotherly types who always have a ready smile and time for a friendly chat too, which sometimes is exactly what you may need.

Although hospitals provide meals for your sick child, they have no obligation to feed a resident parent or other family members, even other children. It can be a very difficult task to have to leave your child's bedside to feed yourself and your other children, but it is essential.

Is there a hospital shop?

Where is it?

What does it stock?

Does it sell things like sandwiches or other eat-on-the-go snacks?

Does it have a good range of children's treats, comics, snacks or toys?

I've always found that when one child is in hospital it's not the time to be too strict about sweets and treats for any of them. A hospital shop with a good selection of sweets and other goodies can make the whole thing much more enjoyable and bearable for everyone. These shops often sell basic children's toys, colouring books, pens, pencils as well as children's comics and magazines. All my children have very happy recollections of virtually every hospital shop we've encountered, remembering them as very special Aladdin's cave types of places.

What about local shops?

How far away are they – how long would it take to walk to them?

What sort of things do they sell?

Hopefully the hospital shop will stock a range of toiletries and sanitary products, but they can't stock everything you might need. If there aren't shops in the immediate vicinity that you can escape to quickly (and sometimes you just go completely stir-crazy if you don't escape sometimes). It can help if you make a list as soon as you can of things to ask friends and relatives to bring in for you.

Useful resources within the hospital

Other useful information to find out is where the PALS office is located within the hospital. PALS stands for The Patient Advice and Liaison Service, a place where you feel that, whatever else is going on, the staff are there for you and are on your side. They are the people to go to if you aren't happy with any aspect of your child's care or treatment, and they can also give you a lot of other information that may make your stay in hospital that little bit easier.

If there is something bothering you about your child's care, as I've already said in Chapter 8, I would advise that you do everything possible to avoid making a formal complaint, but if you really are left with no alternative, PALS are there to support you and advocate for you. Sometimes, though, you might just need a sounding board, and PALS staff are generally excellent at helping you work out how to get better treatment for your child without necessarily making a formal complaint.

Another place that I find to be an oasis of calm is the hospital chapel. These days they are multi-faith, or no faith, very calm spaces, where I find I can sit and just let the stressful thoughts wander around my brain until they eventually settle down and things seem clearer. The chapel is genuinely open to everyone, and it tends to be a very therapeutic place, away from the constant activity of a busy hospital.

Your Visitor Support Network

You can't do this all on your own. Your other children need you, and you need proper breaks from the relentless responsibility of caring for a seriously ill child in a tiny area around a confined bed-space. Now is the time to really call for help. Friends, family, partners, neighbours, anyone you trust, see if they would be willing to take part in a rota at the bedside. Ideally, can anyone do an overnight shift? Over years of being in hospital round the clock with a very poorly Toby, I soon learnt my own limit, after three nights consecutively I start to lose the plot and I begin to want to climb the walls in frustration. Although in reality there have been many periods when I've barely left his bedside for several weeks at a time.

If you can organise a rota of people who you and your child like and trust, and who are also willing to give you a break every now and again, everything will seems much more manageable and less stressful.

It's not as hard as people think it might be, and they won't be expected to take on the full responsibility for your child's care, because the nurses are there to do any complicated medical stuff. All you need from your rota team is a willingness to keep your child company, to help them stay calm and happy. You should leave strict instructions, of course, to ring you if there are any changes or decisions being made in your absence, but other than that, you should be able to escape for a little while and try to sort out your own head every now and again.

There have been numerous periods of 5 or 6 days on the trot when I have been unable to leave Toby's bedside for more than a few moments. Sleeping alongside his bed on a pull-out camp-bed is just about doable, so is the wall-climbing boredom and frustration, but what's really hard is having nowhere to wash, no change of clothes, and no access to proper regular meals or drinks. It's worth asking friends if they would be happy to sit with your child once or twice a week to allow you to at least get home for a couple of hours and touch base with things, have a proper shower in your own bathroom and pack a bag of clean clothes for the next few days, too.

Not everyone will be happy to take on the responsibility of being on the rota, but instead would still like to come and visit you and your child. Welcome them with open arms because it's still lovely to see anyone who can come in to visit. Cooped up together in a side room for days turning into weeks and sometimes turning into months, Toby and I sometimes just needed someone else to pop in and say hello, and a friendly face to change the dynamics a bit too.

People often want to know what to bring, so make a list before you talk to them. Obviously, things that your child would enjoy and which would allay their boredom, but also things for you, or things that both of you need. One very important thing people can bring in is food you can keep by the bedside to snack on; many times things have been so fraught that I've been unable to leave Toby to go and buy food for myself, sometimes I've had nothing to eat for over 24 hours.

My list for me always went something like this:-

Food - Biscuits, apples, oranges, bananas, grapes, a sandwich if you're ravenous.

Things to do - a newspaper just so you can see what's going on in the world, preferably one with a decent crossword and other pen and paper games.

Pen and Paper – because it's so annoying to wake up in the middle of the night with a great idea to ask the doctors, and nowhere to write it down so you have forgotten in by the morning.

Things to cheer you up and make you laugh - I had a friend who always brought me a tiny quarter bottle of red wine every time she came to visit. I'm sure alcohol wasn't allowed on the children's ward, but I wasn't silly enough to ask permission. Somehow the forbidden nature of my naughty little treat, and making sure I was drinking it secretly without getting caught, made it seem much more deliciously enjoyable when it was late into the night and Toby was asleep.

Small Change – there's nothing worse than popping down to the hospital restaurant in the middle of the night and there, in the vending machine is exactly that sandwich that will totally hit the spot.... and you only have notes, and none of the coins that fit the machine.

The Doctor's Round

Once a day, normally in the morning, a whole team of doctors will surround your child's bedside. There is normally a Consultant, at least one Registrar, a few Senior House Officers, maybe a variety of non-specific senior and junior medics too, and perhaps even a medical student. I've listed the ranks vaguely in order of seniority, the Consultant being the Big Cheese.

You really need to be there, to hear what is going on and what decisions are being made about diagnostic tests, procedures or treatment for your child. The junior doctors are sometimes put on the spot as are the medical students, by the Consultant asking their opinion, or their diagnosis. These ward-rounds are a very important part of a junior doctor's on-going training.

When you have a child like Toby, with a medical condition completely unique to himself, you really do need all your wits about you. You also need every ounce of tact, diplomacy and good manners too.

With even the very best will in the world, not even the most committed doctors have the time to go through the full medical history of a child with a complex condition, numerous previous admissions or with multiple disabilities. In our local hospital alone, Toby's notes span eight huge files and need a trolley to move them around. He's also been in countless other hospitals too, each with yet more enormous files. So Toby's complete set of medical records are scattered across several hospitals, no doctor would ever get access to read them all even if they did have the time and resources to do so.

However, there is one person who can remember nearly every detail of all your child's previous hospital admissions, treatments and outcomes, and I'm afraid that person is you.

However, you are not a doctor, so you are unlikely to be asked for your opinion while they are examining your child during their ward-round. I've learnt to interject oh so politely, judging the precisely correct moment. By doing so, I know I can save them loads of time, and I also know I can save Toby from being subjected to invasive procedures that have been tried previously with little or no success. This not only protects Toby from unnecessary distress, but it will also save the hospital money. However, as well as all that saving, I also have to ensure I save the face of the Consultant, who won't be best pleased to be shown up in front of his whole team, whose judgement is being questioned by a wrung-out, sleep-deprived, unwashed mother with the demented look in her eye of someone who hasn't seen the outside world for nearly a week.

The brave new world of modern medicine isn't yet ready for a know-it-all mother. Over the past 20 or 30 years, hospital doctors have become significantly more approachable, but they still have a long way to go. Bear in mind too, that most Paediatric Consultants are dealing with parents of exceedingly healthy, normally developing children, who are in hospital for the one big health scare of their entire childhood, and once some extreme diagnosis has been completely ruled out, they are likely to be sent home by tomorrow, and back at school the following day.

This cohort of very lucky parents don't have the history of hospital admissions that we acquire, they aren't in hospital long enough to see the things that can and do go wrong, and they are so understandably grateful that their child is going to make a complete recovery that they tend to treat every doctor they meet like God, only slightly more important.

Consultants in particular like that a lot.

What they like less are parents like me, the one person standing in the room right now who knows exactly what worked the last time my child was this ill, and what went pear-shaped when a different group of doctors also didn't want to listen to the mother who knows her child's complete medical history.

Most Consultants also are used to treating children with reasonably commonplace ailments, not children like Toby who virtually re-write their own medical textbooks. So when a child like Toby has a mother like me, you can see the confusion in their eyes, because, quite frankly, no matter how softly and gently I speak, or how much I smile they pick up on my knowledge and experience, and they feel challenged. That's often a totally new experience and they really don't like it. Add in the fact that I have been living rough for days on end by the side of a hospital bed and look like something that even the cat wouldn't want to bring in, and they are probably unnerved.

Doctors generally come across two types of parents. Those who think all doctors are gods, and those who shout abuse and thump the table. I've met a few of the table thumpers, and once I saw an irate father forcibly pull out intravenous drips from his child's arms, pick him up and run towards the lift yelling "I'm taking him to a proper hospital where he'll see a proper doctor". Ten minutes later, security guards carried the child back to the ward, and the father wasn't allowed to visit again. So if they meet lovely parents and difficult parents, where do parents like me fit? The parents who deal with some fairly heavy duty medication every day at home and use some pretty high-tech equipment to go with it. The ones who know how to do CPR and have actually had to use it on their own child, the ones who understand the process of infection, disease and disability, or at least the ones that most commonly affect our children.

I want to work with the doctors. I believe firmly in partnership working, that outcomes are better when parents and professionals, in this instance the doctors, pull together and pool all their knowledge and experience for the good of the child. It's very hard to do partnership working all by yourself. It's a bit like doing ballroom dancing on your own.

So even if I choose impeccable timing, whisper softly my thoughts and concerns, and smile as sweetly as I know how, there is often a silence where you expect the Queen of Hearts to appear and point at you and shout "Off with her head". If you watch the doctors carefully during this silence, despite the professional facade of cool calmness they wear so well, their eyes are often betraying complete panic as they try to process their thoughts and decide which of the two types of parents I might possibly be. Well by speaking up I'm obviously unaware that they like to be treated like God, so instead, hey ho, I must be the difficult parent.

I know I'm not being totally fair, and I have met some very senior doctors who are excellent, and who have really gone out of their way to seek my opinions and then act on them, but I can tell you exactly who they are. They are usually the Doctors who didn't listen to me the first time they met me, and they remember the catalogue of catastrophic events that each time led to Toby's condition deteriorating to alarming levels as a direct result of assuming I was just another difficult parent.

My all-time favourite consultant was a difficult old so-and-so to begin with, until things once went so wrong despite my warnings of what was likely to happen. He then wrote a note on the front of Toby's hospital notes stating that, whatever time of day or night Toby arrived in the Accident and Emergency Department, he was to be called immediately at home, and until he could be reached, A & E staff were to do everything Toby's mother suggested. Sometimes you really do want to hug people like that and take them home with you.

The Third Type of Parent

Doctors simply don't have the opportunities often enough to meet medically aware parents of children with disabilities. In cases like Toby's, where he is unique, of course I am going to be more knowledgeable about the details of how his symptoms affect him. The best doctors welcome this knowledge and experience; the more insecure ones are threatened by it.

Doctors are scientists. Some have an excellent bedside manner, many do not. Their role is to cure our children, not to charm the pants off their parents. The medical profession is making remarkably forward-thinking moves towards improving communications and relationships, but it will take at least a generation of doctors before we can expect the cultural shift that's needed. A shift that will ensure that every single doctor/patient/parent conversation is open and two-way, and accepts that if all parties work collaboratively, pulling together and working on the same side with no divide, great things will happen. Time, money, and most importantly of all, lives will be saved, again and again.

Misunderstandings happen, as do mistakes. The problem with the medical profession is that when these misunderstandings and mistakes occur, there can be a closing of ranks against the non-professionals, even if they are a family who are expert in the care of their own child.

Once the ranks are closed there is virtually no way back in.

This is what we each have to guard against. So I would suggest strongly that you never thump tables, raise your voice or swear. However, I never did any of that either. I think I fell foul of the system more often in the early days simply because of what a mother's instinct was telling me loudly and clearly seemed so flipping obvious to me that I honestly believed that as doctors, they would have picked up on what was going on ages before that instinct kicked in. I now know that parents often have a "sixth sense", a clear insight into what's going on, that is completely invisible and lost to everyone else, no matter how much medical training they've undergone.

I was pointing out as obvious something that they simply could not see, not just once, but again and again and again. By doing so, I virtually gave them permission to label me as a "difficult parent".

"Difficult Parent" is one of those labels that will stick and stick, and is very hard to get rid of once it's been given to you. People talk about your child's case, they write notes on everything, using little euphemisms too that allow their colleagues to read between the lines without putting anything so slanderous in their notes or emails that you could take them to task over. Little things like "anxious mother". That's not a lie, I've yet to meet any mother of any hospitalised child that hasn't experienced a moment of anxiety at some point or another, but the writing down of it may imply a much more dismissive meaning to your child's multidisciplinary team.

Once you have lost credibility, being an effective advocate for your child is practically impossible. Retaining credibility and trust is sometimes like walking on eggshells, and it becomes really difficult when you don't feel your child is being treated properly, or you know that what you are saying is not being heard and taken seriously.

It's a very thin line to tread, and is made even harder because you are in such an emotionally charged situation, with a severely ill child. There have been many many times when I have an instinct as to exactly what was wrong with Toby, an instinct that many days or even weeks later would be confirmed as having been correct. Yet I'm watching the medical team completely flummoxed and barking up the wrong tree with tests and procedures that are quite inappropriate. If I am too outspoken in stating my thoughts to them I will quickly get labelled as a difficult parent.

The way I sometimes describe it to others is this. Imagine that a team of doctors have a clipboard with a checklist of 100 steps towards a diagnosis. They start at number 1 and carefully work their way all the way to 100 to figure out what's wrong with somebody. I'm running ahead of them, and up to a point they can understand that not only have I been with Toby when he's been seriously ill before, but also that I have a mother's instinct about him. So if I get to number 14 and wave furiously back to them where they are standing and studying number one or number two, they may take me seriously. However, if I've raced all the way to step number 84 and I'm convinced that I've found the answers, and they are still examining number two, they simply won't be able to accept that I'm so far ahead of them despite my lack of medical training and expertise. I've learnt to be patient, respectful, mindful of their sensibilities and very subtle too. If I shout out what I think it might be too soon, I'll lose all credibility and alienate them. Toby needs me on the same side as the doctors, so I've learnt to bide my time.

Meanwhile, he is often worsening before my very eyes. Doing it this way means that when they are ready to hear me they will listen. Doing it the wrong way means that I might never get to help them find a way to make him better.

Doctors and experienced, medical-savvy parents come from very different places. Doctors have been trained to work in a way that is careful, methodical, scientific and evidence-based. Parents often have highly- tuned gut-instincts. I understand that I cannot expect a doctor who has only known me a few days to understand that my gut-instincts are often spot-on, and to take a wager on the fact that I may be right. How on earth can he or she tell whether I'm a crackpot eccentric or not? I often have no scientific tangible way of explaining how I arrived at my hypothesis, I just "know". To them, it would sound as bizarre as if I told them I'd read it in the stars. However, knowing and understanding all this doesn't mean it's any less frightening and frustrating, while I'm waiting for them to be ready to listen.

Keeping your child calm and happy in hospital

How do you keep a very ill child happy and occupied for long periods in hospital? Even extremely ill children can very easily become bored, frightened and fractious.

On the ward there may be access to a Play Therapist, who can help set up things for your child to do at their bedside. It's great if your child naturally likes books or colouring or similar things. Lots of children, as we all know, are hooked up almost 24/7 to their mobile devices or internet tablets. There may or may not be easily accessed internet on the ward, but it's worth checking.

Most hospitals have bedside TV sets on brackets above each bed. The best of these systems also have a computer screen function too. Normally patients have to pay for them, but many hospitals waive the charges for their children's ward. It is worth asking if that's the case on your child's ward.

The small area around your child's bed or cot very quickly becomes your second home. With imagination, you can customise that tiny area in all sorts of ways to make it feel more welcoming.

Things I do include tying helium balloons onto the bed but within Toby's reach so he can pull the ribbon down to grab the balloon, then let it bounce upwards again. I stick pictures and photos of the people he loves around the bed where he can see them easily.

Your child may also be quite miffed to discover that there are teachers in hospitals too! They teach all the school-age children who have been in hospital for at least 3 days. Some larger hospitals have proper schools on the premises, and they really can be excellent. The hospital teachers liaise with your child's own school so they can set appropriate schoolwork. Children get the benefit of being kept occupied for at least part of every day, it can give you a much needed break too, they may get the opportunity to enjoy being with other children, and they are less likely to fall behind their peer-group at school.

When we were living at Guys Hospital for several months while Toby was an in-patient, I managed to enrol Francesca into the hospital school on a resident sibling basis. She was only five at the time, but now, many years later, she still has happy vibrant memories of her time there.

The hospital school experience can also give your child much needed respite from the whole "being poorly" aspect of being in hospital. As far as possible school-time is ring-fenced so that blood tests, investigations or visits from doctors and nurses are kept to an absolute minimum during school times, so your child may feel that their school-time is a safe haven away from the things that they are having to cope with on the ward.

Minimising the trauma

Your child may have to undergo a whole battery of procedures, tests and investigations and some may need to be repeated several times whilst they are in hospital. Blood tests are often a particularly frequent experience that can be traumatic for some children, and often for their parents as well.

Blood tests are necessary, but I sometimes question whether the frequency of them is always totally necessary or not. Please don't be afraid to ask how important a test actually is. Many times, I've managed to negotiate fewer deeply unpleasant procedures on Toby's behalf.

There is often a basic assumption that my role is to help in cajoling my child to submit to a blood test or other nastinesses, and I have often been expected to help the staff restrain Toby while they do whatever they have to do. Over the years I have realised that I don't want to be a part of that experience for Toby. As his mother, I firmly believe that my role as a resident parent is to support him, not the staff. If supporting him conflicts with what the staff need to do, it's at these times when I need to be his ally, not part of the team administering the unpleasant experiences.

For me this is quite a big issue, because I remember vividly my terror at being held down in hospital as a small child while they stuck needles in me. It has left me with a life-long needle-phobia, and inadvertently, I have given Toby every opportunity to pick up on my very real fears every time we have faced his blood-tests together.

Every parent will feel differently about these issues, but I think it's important to be true to what you feel is right for you and your child, and you should also be able to discuss your feelings with the staff.

An equally valid viewpoint that many parents take is that this is an unpleasant thing to happen, so that by helping to hold their child still they are speeding up the process and getting it over and done with more quickly.

Over the years, Toby has also faced several anaesthetics. It is common practice now for a parent to be allowed to stay with their child all the way to theatre, right up to the moment when the anaesthetic is working and your child is asleep. It doesn't matter how many times you see this happen to your child, it is always distressing to see them succumb to the anaesthetic, and become lifeless and floppy.

For many years, Toby was so ill and his health was so volatile that they wouldn't contemplate anaesthetising him unless there was an available intensive care bed ready and waiting. That often meant that we would be blue-lighted in an ambulance to a distant hospital with the relevant intensive care availability. There was always a very real, but unspoken, possibility that Toby might not wake up again after the anaesthetic, and these were very frightening times when I felt particularly vulnerable.

There is nothing else to do when your child is in theatre but to worry yourself crazy and hope and pray that everything will be all right. It's very rare for it not to be, but worrying yourself silly unfortunately is a huge part of parenting any child, let alone one with the extra problems our children face.

I've never had to deal with those long periods of waiting on my own, there has always been someone else with me, and I feel desperately sorry for parents who don't have that support. I normally drink copious amounts of coffee in the hospital canteen, but no matter how long the procedure takes, I have never been able to leave the hospital building during that time.

There are various things I can do that I've worked out make the whole thing seem a little bit more bearable. Firstly, both the surgeon and the anaesthetist always come and see you and your child beforehand. I am always charm-personified.... I know it sounds crazy but I always think that if they like you they are more likely to take good care of your child. I know they will anyway, but it's just a little bit of extra belt-and-braces superstition for me.

Secondly, I always ask the anaesthetist if he can deliver the anaesthetic via a face-mask, which they have always agreed to do. It's not something that they routinely tell parents about, generally you have to ask if it's possible, and in our experience, it's a much more gentle, calm way of doing it than having a cannula fitted into a vein. However, some anaesthetists are less keen to use face-masks, and I have also been told that some children panic with them. However, most children panic at the idea of having a needle into their arm too, to fit a cannula. They will still need to fit a cannula because they will need vein access while your child is asleep, but they can easily insert it later in theatre.

Once your child is taken to theatre, things happen very quickly. It always seems like the room is jam-packed with people, and everyone is gowned up wearing hats and masks, so that can be quite a culture shock if you're not prepared for it. Apart from one nurse who normally comes from the ward with your child, the whole team are theatre staff, so you won't know them, but that doesn't normally matter because I am always struck by the total gentle kindness from everybody, towards Toby and towards me.

Before you know it, your child is asleep, and you are being ushered out of the room. Another little superstitious ritual of mine is to always plead "Now you will take care of him for me, won't you please, because he really is very special". OK so I'm totally over the top, but it helps me feel I've done everything I possibly can to protect him.

As you leave the room, you may feel a bit wobbly or even tearful, but there is another important thing to negotiate before you can even think about falling apart.

After any operation, all patients are taken to a side ward near the theatre which is called the "Recovery Room". This is where your child will be closely monitored as the anaesthetic begins to wear off and they wake up. Often, parents don't gain access to the recovery room, but have to wait until later on to be reunited with their child, when they are brought back to the ward.

I never wanted Toby to wake up alone in the recovery room with people he didn't know, so, before leaving the Theatre Department, I always did what I could to persuade them to let me be there, in the Recovery Room, before he woke up.

There are very good reasons why the staff are reticent to allow it; your child may still have breathing tubes in their mouths or up their nostrils, there may be blood-stains on your child's skin or bedclothes, basically, it often isn't a pretty sight, and the staff have enough to do with ensuring your child's medical safety straight after an operation without having to reassure freaked-out parents.

So although you're feeling wobbly and untogether and biting back the tears, you somehow have to convince them that you are totally laid-back about things, you've been there and done it a thousand times before, and you'll be an asset to the team rather than a liability. So far, I have always managed to persuade them to let me in. You may need to be persistent, but it is possible to persuade them to let you be there so that your face is the first one your child will see when they wake up.

For me this feels like the right thing to do, but it may not feel the same for you. So think about how you feel and what you want. There are several half-way measures too – perhaps ask to be called just before they take your child back to the ward so you can be with them while they are being moved, or maybe have a special soft-toy of your child's, and ask the staff to give it to them the minute they wake up. Try to negotiate whatever you think would be best for you and your child.

The thing is, hospitals have their rules and procedures, and a lot of these are in place to make their working day easier, rather than for the patient's benefit. Parents with children like ours are a lot more hospital-savvy than most, and I think it's appropriate to request that sometimes, the rules are stretched just that little bit for children who really have to contend with a load more than most.

The Photos

One other little thing I always do is to bring some really good photos of Toby into the hospital, preferably really happy-looking ones which are shining with personality. I either pin them close to his bed in a prominent place where staff can see them easily, or have them in a small album but showing them to as many staff as often as I can.

When Toby is ill, he becomes a shadow of his usual self, but staff don't know how he is normally, and often assume that he's like this all the time. They meet a Toby who is gaunt, fragile, sad, silent and withdrawn, and they just can't envisage the spirited, boisterous, mischievous, hilarious, warm, loud out-going whirlwind of a character that he normally is. All they know is that he is profoundly disabled, and many have been surprised to hear that he can even actually walk.

Showing photos of Toby at his best has paid off time and time again. It helps the staff recognise that Toby, despite his disabilities, has a quality of life and a presence that is completely life-enhancing. Seeing the photos has a really positive effect on the staff, they warm towards him, they realise how very ill he must be feeling, and there is often a perceptible extra layer of goodwill towards him. The unspoken message is clear – "Toby has a great life, and a huge number of people who love him. He may be disabled, but his life is precious and worth fighting tooth and nail for".

TIPS, TRICKS AND STRATEGIES

This is crisis time, you need help, work out who you can call on to support you.

Work out exactly what support you need.

Do everything you possibly can to stay overnight, every night with your child.

Sort out the practicalities, food, drink, showers for yourself.

Make sure you have small change for vending machines.

Do not be intimidated by the staff, particularly on the doctor's ward round.

You may know more than they are giving you credit for, but don't come across as a know-it-all.

Good manners and cheerfulness at all times can be hard, but it helps get the staff on your side.

Do whatever it takes to keep your child happy.

Speak up for your child. Question very nicely the necessity for each and every invasive test that is planned for them.

Bring a photo or a photo album of your child looking their happiest best, and put it somewhere where all staff will easily see it. Otherwise they don't know what your child is really like. A good photo turns a patient into a person in the eyes of the staff.

Don't forget your mobile phone charger!

CHAPTER 10
Hospital Appointments

For a family like ours who have spent far too much time actually staying in hospitals, the additional constant stream of hospital appointments can also be a real chore at times. Throughout Toby's childhood, we averaged around 40 hospital out-patient appointments every year, and because the other two children also had their fair share of out-patient appointments, it was a very rare week that we were "hospital-free".

At one time we were regularly seeing 14 separate Consultants on Toby's behalf; a General Paediatrician at our local hospital, a specialist Paediatrician at Guys, a Respiratory Specialist, a Cardiologist, an Immunologist, a Psychiatrist, an Orthopaedic Surgeon, a General Surgeon, an Audiologist, an Opthalmologist, a Gastroenterologist, a Geneticist, a Dermatologist and a Burns Specialist.

I'm exhausted just writing them all down, and these are just the doctors. Toby also regularly saw the Surgical Appliance department for specialist footwear, physiotherapy, speech and language therapy, occupational therapy.... the list goes on and on. Each time I had to drive to collect Toby from school, struggling to lift his heavy wheelchair into the boot with all his feeding equipment and nappy changing bag, then after driving to the hospital, circling the perimeter road several times until a disabled parking space became free, getting the wheelchair and peripheral equipment out of the boot, persuading Toby to get out of the car and into the wheelchair (I'm not joking when I tell you that sometimes we missed our appointment slot simply because he thought it was hilarious to refuse to get out of the car), then push him to the right department and keep him occupied in the waiting room.

In paediatric out-patients, over-running clinics are fairly normal, and it's not unusual to have to keep Toby happy for well over an hour before we can be seen. How? Normally, to my acute embarrassment, the only way of keeping him calm and happy without a TV to watch was by me singing an endless stream of nursery rhymes and action songs with the enthusiasm and jollity of an over-zealous children's TV presenter. You can imagine how other parents would give us an extremely wide berth.

Toby is a one-off, and his health used to be hopelessly fragile and volatile until he was about ten years old, so we have always been fortunate enough to be given an allocated appointment time with the "Main Man", the Consultant themselves. Generally, we also had a full 30 minute clinic appointment allocation, but by the time we entered the room I would be exhausted, embarrassed, flustered and on the verge of tears of frustration. Toby, too, would also be at the end of his rope, wanting to explore the room, clear the doctor's desk of any paperwork on it, and determined to rifle through any drawers or cupboards in a focused mission to create a one-boy wave of destruction.

Generally, this doesn't augur well for meetings, particularly the ones when you really want to create an impression of being in control and cool, calm and collected. It's very difficult to retain credibility in these situations or to even approach anything like partnership working so that you can get the best outcomes for the health of your child. You just have to accept that all you can do is the best that you can in the circumstances you are presented with.

We had too many hospital appointments for me to always be able to bring another adult who could at least keep Toby occupied while I had a sensible discussion with the doctor. At some appointments, it was all discussion among adults, with not even the most cursory medical examination of Toby. I sometimes wondered why I had gone to all the stress and trouble of collecting Toby from school with all his equipment, and kept him happy in the waiting room at huge personal cost to my exhaustion levels. We would have achieved much more in our adult discussion than was possible while I was also trying to keep Toby's behaviour under control. However, I knew that to suggest such an option would have probably created entirely the wrong impression, and wouldn't have gone down very well.

Over time I got much better at handling these consultations, and a lot of it is down to planning. It's always a good idea to have a ready prepared list of questions or topics you'd like to cover with the doctor, and I now start preparing those questions several days beforehand, asking for the opinions of other people too – school staff, the school medical team, other therapists, carers, close family and friends. Asking for input from others who know him well sometimes brings up issues I was completely unaware of, and it helps get my head around the important issues and focus my mind better.

If there is any way someone else can come to the meetings jump at the offer – it won't always be possible, but it certainly takes the pressure off enormously when you have a bit of back-up.

I always take Toby's prescription list of medicines with me – because remembering the whole long list of nearly 20 items when you're put on the spot is nigh on impossible.

I also developed other strategies to cope with these constant meetings. One thing I found very helpful was to work out the purpose and the importance of each meeting. Then I could try and work out what I wanted each meeting to achieve for Toby.

I also eventually learnt to take control of the diary. I would ring the out-patient department every few months and reschedule as many appointments as possible to ensure I got a completely appointment-free week at least once every six weeks. I would also try and make sure as many as possible of the appointment times were at times to suit me rather than the hospital. The round-trip from our house to Toby's school and then on to the hospital was 25 miles, and took 90 minutes, including loading and unloading Toby and all his equipment in and out of the car. So unless appointments were at either end of the school day rather than slap-bang in the middle, Toby would invariably miss a whole day's school. Occasionally I was really lucky and managed to book more than one appointment on the same day, which made life immeasurably easier.

This exercise felt like I was taking back a little bit of control over the whole outpatient's situation. Up until that point, I had felt like

I always had to be there whenever they snapped their fingers to summon our attendance, constantly dancing to the hospital's tune whenever their piper wanted to play.

It's like a misunderstanding of epic proportions, because the medical teams offering all these appointments felt that by doing so they were being supportive and helpful, and in some ways they were, but often it was just too much for me to cope with.

Sadly, over time, it becomes more and more apparent that even during a 30 minute consultation, a doctor doesn't get a chance to get a real feel for who Toby is, what he can do, and where his strengths and limitations lie. Even in purely medical terms, they can only ever get a snapshot – they can't be in our house in the middle of the night when he is so ill he can barely breathe, or understand fully his pattern of gastrostomy-related occasional vomiting. Particularly with a child like Toby, who is so much of one-off, it can be really hard for Consultants to add much to the equation about his condition.

That is not to say that all these meetings are a waste of time, in fact they can be enormously helpful, but only if you are aware of what the parameters are, what you want out of the meeting, and understand the limitations of what is possible.

What every parent in my situation really wants is a doctor to find the magic solution, and make all their child's difficulties better in an instant. Well, that's never going to happen. When you have a child who is unique, there is no research budget whatsoever to even begin to get to the bottom of the medical mysteries that is their make-up, and even if there was, it would take years of unravelling and discoveries to make even a tiny bit of difference.

So, what can Consultants do for families like ours? Well, they can review, check, and listen and suggest things if you describe new symptoms or any new concerns, which can be very reassuring. They can also act as a sounding board, and help you gain a better perspective on your child's condition and symptoms. They can write letters on your child's behalf to help secure funding from other statutory services or charity grants. They can make referrals to other specialists regarding new or worsening symptoms, and they can keep you up to date on any new medical breakthroughs and research which may shed more light on your child's condition.

They can also prescribe new medication, and sometimes it has felt as if they have hit the medication jackpot button, and when that happens, it can make an enormous difference.

We have had some real Eureka life-changing decisions made during outpatient appointments. When that happens, it makes all the times I've been stressed out and exhausted by the appointment-treadmill seem worthwhile. You simply just never quite know when something incredible is about to happen.

There are four particularly life-changing appointments I remember so well, that I have almost total technicolour and surround-sound recall of them. During each of these appointment, a different, but particularly tuned-in Consultant had a moment of insight into our lives, and responded by recommending a new drug for Toby to try. In each case, these drugs simply transformed our lives for the better.

Each time though, it felt like it was a bit of a lottery as to whether the decision would be made to recommend these drugs or not. If each particular doctor hadn't had their particular "light-bulb" moment at that particular time, we could have been left struggling indefinitely.

I'm not recommending any of these drugs for any other child, I am only naming them to enable me to demonstrate the huge positive impact each had on Toby's well-being. There may be drugs that could provide solutions for your child too, that maybe you've never heard of, and none of your medical team has thought to try yet. Sometimes it can pay to talk to other parents about their child's medication, or to research things yourself on the internet. If you find out about any medication that might help in your child's situation, you may then be able to talk it over with your child's Consultant as to whether or not it might be appropriate.

Singulair

At an appointment at Guys Hospital, a few months after Toby had finally been discharged from his marathon 8 month stay, we went back to see the Consultant who had been in charge of his care. It felt like going back to see a very old and trusted friend.

It was late summer, 1998, and a new drug had just been launched which was still very new, and not licenced for children at this stage at all. However the Consultant asked if we would be willing to try it for Toby, since it seemed to work really well on certain lung conditions. Toby was four years old at the time, weak and frail from his continued battle with serious chest infections. There really wasn't much to lose, since we knew Toby had already exceeded his projected life-expectancy, and we were also under no illusions that, next time, ventilation could not be considered because each time he had been ventilated to save his life, the process had caused further irreparable damage to his already diseased lungs, and we knew that he wouldn't survive another ventilation attempt.

So we said yes, and came home with a packet of little pink tablets. First problem. The instructions said they have to be chewed. Toby can't chew. So I crushed them, and flushed them through his gastrostomy tube.

Within about 48 hours Toby was different. Somehow more energetic, with colour in his cheeks for the first time ever, and a presence about him that somehow glowed of cheekiness. That night, I noticed that his laboured breathing was quieter. I held my breath as always that winter, and he was only admitted twice to hospital, and each time responded to treatment really quickly in a way he never had before.

I'm not a pharmacist and I don't really know what the chemical make-up of Singulair is, but I do know that one of the ingredients must be magic.

Best of all, from that day to this, he has never needed to be ventilated since.

When he was 15, another Consultant wanted to take him off these daily wonder-pills. NOOOOO I pleaded. Yes, said the Consultant. We compromised and I agreed to trying him off them as long as we waited until the end of the winter months.

I held my breath all summer and most of the following winter, but Toby sailed through, rosy cheeked and full of life. He simply doesn't need them anymore.

Melatonin

Toby becoming energetic was very much a double-edged sword. It meant he never wanted to sleep. You can kind of understand it, this kid had spent so much of his life in hospital desperately ill he didn't want to waste a moment in a boring bed in the semi-dark when there was a wonderful world to explore and create havoc in. So he simply resisted any bedtime attempt whatsoever.

Bedtimes became a complete nightmare. I'd put him into bed, he'd slide out of bed, I'd lie next to him, he'd climb over me, I'd turn the music off, he'd scream his head off. This would often go on until about three or four in the morning, and eventually I'd just leave him in his bedroom watching TV so at least I got a couple of hours sleep before I'd have to get up at 6am to start his morning medical care regime before school. I was a zombie, and the whole street was rocking to the sound of the Tweenies all night long. It escalated when he got to about 10 or 11, and the resistance became violent too. Putting him to bed resulted in bruises and scratches all over the place, and I was beyond my wits end.

I had mentioned this to every single doctor we saw between the time this started when he was about 6 right up until he was nearly 13. Then we saw a new Consultant, and I told her how our whole lives were being controlled by Toby's bedtime refusal.

"Have you not tried Melatonin?" She said. I'd never even heard of it. Later I found out that a load of my friend's children had been on it for years, and it was quite standard treatment, incredibly safe and effective like you would not believe. This lovely doctor wrote out a prescription so I could leave the hospital with a month-long supply. That night, I dissolved the tablet in water and flushed it down his gastrostomy tube, and less than an hour later he was yawning his head off. We only just managed to get him upstairs in time, I changed his nappy and put his pyjamas on while he was snoring. We have not looked back since. Bedtimes are now a total dream, and he's normally fast asleep having the sweetest of dreams by 10pm every evening.

Prophylactic Antibiotics

Another real breakthrough, suggested by a doctor who really understood the misery of Toby's constant ill-health partly caused by his very low immunity, was prophylactic antibiotics.

Even though the Singulair had worked incredibly well and was preventing really serious chest infections, Toby was still picking up every bug going, and they would always gravitate towards his chest. So although we were keeping him out of hospital, it was largely because I was working really hard and staying up with him all night to keep his chest clear whenever he had a bug. When they were introduced, the prophylactic antibiotics worked almost like a switch, he rarely gets more that one or two difficult few days every year now.

Prophylactic antibiotics are given for 3 days every fortnight, whether he is well or ill, so his body always has a bit of extra "fight" in it on a "just in case" basis, and for Toby, it really has made another huge improvement.

Hyoscine Patches

As you know, Toby doesn't swallow properly, which means that he dribbles for England. As he got older, this became more and more socially unacceptable, and it was beginning to impede his ability to charm the pants off everyone.

At another clinic appointment, a doctor suggested trying Hyoscine Patches, which is a little round patch that is supposed to go behind his ear, and only needs changing every 3 days. Hyoscine is actually an anti-sickness medication, but the patches deliver a very low dose of the drug, just enough to dry up excess secretions.

However, there was big problem. I would put it on him, and he would peel it off. I tried creeping into his bedroom in the middle of the night to put it on him when he wouldn't know; every morning it was peeled off. I asked the doctor if it could go on any other part of his body, and I was told that no, it had to go close to his ear, otherwise it wouldn't work. We gave up, eventually.

A few months later, he needed another anaesthetic, and the anaesthetist was asking about his current medication. When we'd gone through them all, he saw that he had also been written up for these patches and asked why I hadn't mentioned it. We ended up having a long discussion, and he explained that, although they are more effective behind his ear, they should work pretty well anywhere. So we tried again, and now he has them on the small of his back at the very spot he can't possibly reach, and he hardly ever dribbles any more.

The sad thing is that we had given up on the patches. If it hadn't been for a random conversation with that anaesthetist, I would never have re-introduced them. They seem to work very effectively indeed on the small of his back, and he is unaware that they are even there. It's awful to think that there may be many other families who have given up for good because their child didn't tolerate them near their ear, and like I was told initially, they have been led to believe that they won't work elsewhere on the body.

Hyoscine Patches have made a huge difference to Toby's quality of life. People are far more responsive to him now that he no longer has rivers of spittle hanging down from his mouth all the time. He gets stared at far less, and people are warm towards him. Many people can't quite hide their revulsion concerning constant dribbling, and that can have a huge negative impact of the self-esteem of a person with learning disabilities who cannot control their saliva. It's very much an inclusion issue. Other people's attitudes towards dribbling reduce opportunities for people who dribble to take a full part in society, being accepted and visible within their own communities.

Getting the best from these appointments

The other thing that outpatient appointments can do is support you in gaining access to other services and equipment, or supporting your case to achieve a better care-package for your child. A letter with a Paediatric Consultant's name at the bottom opens doors, it really does, and so building goodwill and strong relationships with the senior members of you child's medical team can really make a difference to the quality of your child's life.

Also, it can be useful to talk to them about the management of your child's conditions. Over the years, not only does your child get older and maybe stronger which means that the drug doses may need to be increased, but treatments and therapies change too. Make sure you mention every intervention you are currently doing with your child every time you see the relevant consultant, because otherwise you could be delivering care in a way that is outmoded and possibly no longer appropriate now they are much bigger and older.

Go through all the medications your child is currently on – as your child gets older there may be drugs that work better that are worth trying.

I often felt that the way the out-patient appointment system works is very wasteful, both of the hospital resources and of my time and energy. Instead of seeing so many different people, it would have made so much more sense to turn up once every two or three months and see either a whole team together, or just one Consultant who had a clear brief from all the others as to what they wanted to check on, and he or she would then be responsible for taking on the whole examination.

A lot of the time, a phone-call would have worked just as well as a full-blown appointment, In fact in terms of being able to engage in an intelligent conversation without trying to restrain Toby from causing havoc at the same time, a phone-call would often have achieved far more, with much less stress all around. Doing it this way would also probably save the NHS enormous sums of money too.

The NHS is lagging far behind most other organisations in embracing the digital revolution to enhance communication. Although they are getting better, trying to get a direct email address for a particular doctor is like trying to find the Holy Grail, it can be virtually impossible. Yet it would make life so much easier if parents could email the queries and questions they would like to cover at the appointment ahead of time, and maybe even bypass a clinic appointment altogether by exchanging emails instead. I read something that made my heart dance with joy on this subject recently – there is a small-scale trial in one area of the NHS where consultations are being offered on Skype! So maybe the 21st century will eventually penetrate the NHS after all.

So why do there have to be so many appointments?

Well, there seems to be a diktat within the NHS that if a Consultant doesn't see a particular patient at least once every 12 months, that patient is automatically discharged so that access to that Consultant would have to be requested all over again via the GP. With children like ours that is a fairly crazy way of doing things, because our children may appear to be fine in one particular aspect of their health for a very long time. That very same aspect, though, could then become seriously troublesome several times over in quick succession a couple of years later.

The other difficulty with the way the out-patient system currently works is that it takes a very rare doctor to be able and willing to look at Toby holistically and treat the whole person. Instead, he is regarded as a list of symptoms, often with each one being looked at in isolation. This runs the risk of a medication being prescribed that will have a detrimental effect on another of his symptoms, or a symptom being looked at in isolation without realising that it is part of a much bigger picture.

There are other things that can be helpful to remember when you are dealing with such a large team. It is only human nature that you will "click" with certain Consultants and less so with others. Some will be very key to your child's overall well-being while others may only have a limited impact.

So it helps if you can sort out in your own mind which ones you trust and need most, which ones you regard as a less important "tick-box" experience, and which ones might be able and willing to support you if you really need help with an issue in a different area of your child's life such as social care or education. Try to build allies, do everything you can to get them on your side, and if you can only bring along an extra adult occasionally, try and ensure they come to the most important and potentially valuable meetings.

It also never hurts to be direct and actually ask the doctor for their email addresses or the direct telephone number and name of their personal secretary. Consultant's secretaries can be very good people to have on your side. I've had several times when I've phoned one of these senior secretaries with a real problem about Toby's condition, and they have always gone that extra mile to get me the right answers or to arrange for the right people to ring me back very quickly. Explain to the consultant that you appreciate their input and knowledge, and whilst you would never abuse their trust, it would be helpful to know that you could contact them if a new development occurs. It helps to have an example, for instance, "I wish I'd been able to ask you about that 2 months ago when he first started waking up in the middle of the night".

It's quite interesting to think that these Consultants we see in Outpatients are the very same Consultants who sometimes intimidate and patronise on the ward rounds. Generally speaking, without their audience of junior doctors to impress, they are much more approachable and human in the outpatient setting, and of course, in a full half-hour when it's just them and us, I think they find it easier to listen.

However, even the outpatient's department doesn't change all of them; there are plenty who really do still get it all wrong in the way they deal with parents. I think this is best illustrated by a note I received from a close friend of mine, following a very difficult hospital appointment with her child. Here goes:-

Yvonne, if you ever get a chance to tell the medical profession what parents really want from them, here's my bit.

- *Please really try not to be late for your first appointment with us. My child has autism as well as their other conditions, and can become very distressed by waiting.*
- *Please introduce the other people in the room.*
- *Please listen and look at my child.*
- *Please listen and look at me too.*
- *It would really help if you could have all the notes, arranged in order.*
- *Please could you read the up-to-date notes before we walk in so we don't have to explain the last 13 years every single time we see you.*
- *Please try and develop some empathy, and then learn how to use it. Do you think you could start to use your common-sense, too?*

- *Please pronounce your words clearly.*
- *Please show some basic level of respect to both me and my child.*
- *Please stop just ticking boxes, or at the very least, please make us feel you're not ticking boxes.*
- *Please understand that no matter how bad the person sitting in front of you says it is, it's actually at least ten times worse.*
- *The person in front of you probably never gets anywhere near enough sleep.*
- *The person in front of you doesn't get a day off, a holiday, and will never be able to retire from their job, either.*
- *The person in front of you is neither stupid nor unimportant. Please don't completely ignore non-verbal children.*
- *It really would help enormously if you could lose some of your ego.*
- *Did you know that all the parents you see also talk to each other?*
- *Did you also know that we notice all your inconsistencies and we don't like them much?*
- *It would also really help if you had the courtesy to at least acknowledge my email or letter.*
- *Have you ever thought it might be a good idea to take your head out of your backside because otherwise, you might miss something?*
- *Please don't use my child as your guinea-pig.*
- *Please don't talk to me about the cost of a drug. My child is priceless, so it's irrelevant.*

The above list was posted on Facebook initially. This mother was steaming in a way that probably only other parents of children like ours could totally understand, because we've all had appointments that felt just like this. Other parents of children with disabilities started sharing their stories in the comment boxes, the indignation, rage, frustration and the helplessness tumbled onto the page again and again. The debate ran for days, the pent-up emotions of dozens of parents sharing, supporting, commiserating and finally, doing exactly what we all do best, finding the hilarity in our absurd situation, and laughing about the whole ridiculousness of it all.

When all else fails and you don't think you have the resources, patience, tolerance or time to attend another out-patient appointment ever again, think on this.

When Toby turned 18, slowly, one by one, each of his consultants had to discharge him back to the care of our GP Practice because the NHS doesn't offer the same level of monitoring and care to adults. This in itself was a concern; our GP's barely know Toby because we have always seen a hospital consultant at least every couple of weeks or so. They also can't possibly be expected to have the same breadth and depth of knowledge as a whole team of specialists.

I was further concerned when I realised that the service the GPs offer is a once a year healthcare check for learning disability adults. Going from 40 or so appointments a year down to one felt like going from the sublime to the ridiculous.

TIPS, TRICKS AND STRATEGIES

If at all possible, take someone with you.

Work out beforehand what you want to achieve, so have your questions and issues clear in your own mind.

Talk to other people who know your child well beforehand, and see if there are any concerns you haven't noticed yet.

Take a notepad with you, and write down new information.

Try to get the Consultant's email address or the direct line phone number to their secretary.

Take a current list of your child's medications with you to every appointment.

Find out if it is necessary to bring your child every time, and if so, see if anyone else can come specifically to supervise, so that you can have a proper conversation with the consultant.

Rearrange appointment times to suit you, rather than suiting the hospital.

Don't be afraid to ask for a second opinion if you're not happy. This is something every NHS patient is entitled to have.

Research potential medications yourself, either by chatting to other parents of disabled children who are facing similar issues, or by using the internet to see what may be available. Then you can suggest the drug to the Consultant, who simply may never have thought of it as appropriate, when it may be one of those drugs that actually make a fairly significant difference.

CHAPTER 11
Intensive Care

For any parent, seeing your child in intensive care for the first time is a pretty shocking moment. There may be leads and lines coming out from all sorts of places. If your child is very small, they are likely to be virtually naked apart from a nappy, which makes them look even more vulnerable. They may be ventilated, with a machine making a really unsettling puffing noise as it does your child's breathing for them, and they are likely to be in an induced coma, with drugs keeping them both sedated and paralysed.

There is no preparation for seeing your child like this. Nothing can really prepare you for the sheer terror you feel seeing your child completely dwarfed by high-tech machinery designed to keep them alive. Your mind will run away with you, and you will start fearing the very worst.

Your child, like every other child in nearby beds, is desperately ill, but the vast majority of children admitted to PICU (Paediatric Intensive Care Unit) survive, get through it, and go home to make good recoveries.

If you've never been into PICU before, you may be quite surprised to notice how calm, quiet and controlled everything seems. I think TV has led a lot of people to expect it to be full of dramas and crash teams and constant fervent efforts to save people's lives, but it usually really isn't like that at all. Once a child is on a ventilator, their breathing rhythm is being mechanically controlled and their heart rate closely monitored, so they are relatively safe from the prospect of sudden, unexpected death. The whole aura of the place somehow exudes safeness and care.

Once you get used to it, you actually begin to think that your child simply could not be safer anywhere else in the hospital. Normally, every child in an intensive care bed has a designated specialist nurse sitting at their bedside all the time, monitoring every bleep on every machine, watching over them and constantly checking that all the lights and dials and changing numbers are within safe limits to ensure your child's body continues to function as well as it possibly can. These nurses are highly trained and very experienced. They are also usually some of the nicest staff you could meet.

That's not to say things can't go wrong, and that mistakes never happen. Of course they can and sometimes do. I wish I could say that I had always felt Toby was in the safest of hands, but there have been times when, even in intensive care, he was put at unnecessary risk by human error. His foot was terribly badly burned, disfiguring him for life, during one of his intensive care admissions.

I think it gets harder to trust as you gain more and more experience of hospital procedures, and as you begin to understand your child's condition better. However, I also developed a sixth sense, and there were certain staff, and certain units where I felt Toby really was as safe as he possibly could be, and I was able to lower my guard and trust that the staff would do all in their power to protect him.

PICU staff are very highly trained and experienced, and due to the one-to-one nature of the nursing care, your child should be receiving the very best possible treatment with the latest technology available. I would suggest that you absorb as much as you possibly can about your child's treatment and the technology being used, and that you are at the bedside often enough to keep a watchful eye on things for your own peace of mind. Generally though, you don't need to be at the bedside the whole time; now is the time you can conserve some of your own very precious and over-stretched energy.

Earlier in the day that Toby was brought up to Guy's Hospital, he had been in our local hospital but desperately ill and there had been a frantic ring-round to every hospital far and wide, on the hunt for a vacant paediatric intensive care bed. At last, Guy's agreed to take him, and they also arranged for their own Retrieval Team to come out for him.

It was probably one of the most scary days of my life...... until the Retrieval Team bounced in and took over. They were just incredible, I'd never seen anything quite like it. There were probably only four of them, but they seemed to fill the room. They were like medical Ghostbusters, all in jumpsuits, wearing backpacks and just exuding confidence and skill. It was like watching a world-class team of gymnasts, the way they just silently took their places, pulled out one piece of high tech equipment after another, and danced around the bedside in perfect synchronisation. The local hospital staff had been gently elbowed out of the way, and all of us stood back and watched in awe as they did whatever they did with such ease and panache. These weren't just doctors, they were showmen.

Within a few minutes, they had Toby ventilated, sedated and paralysed, and he was being carried at speed toward the waiting ambulance, with the team all working on him as they drove away, lights flashing, sirens blaring, hurtling through the traffic towards central London. It took several minutes before I could pick my jaw up off the floor, but I just knew, in only the way a parent can know, that he was in safe hands and that I could relax for the first time in weeks.

We had to pop home to arrange longer term child-care for Francesca and Adam, and to collect a few bits and pieces, and then Chris and I drove up to London to find Guy's Hospital and Toby. It would be eight months before I set foot back in through my own front door, but I didn't know that then.

Walking into Intensive Care for the first time, we were ushered through to Toby's cot-side, and seeing him lying there completely still, with dozens of leads and lines flowing in and out of his body, his arms in splints and his breathing being done by a huge machine was too surreal to even be shocking.

We met the nurse who had been caring for Toby for the previous couple of hours. He was gentle, kind and knowledgeable and just exuded confidence and trust. He firstly showed me the best place to sit to be able to hold Toby's motionless hand, organised a cup of tea, and then explained very calmly exactly what each piece of equipment was doing, and why it was necessary. He listened and answered every question, he explained things over and over again until I had grasped most of it, and I was able to breathe easily, because someone so able was caring for Toby. It felt to me as if this man was Toby's very own Guardian Angel.

Intensive care has a totally different feel to a normal ward. All the children are completely silent and still. There is an intensity of care, but delivered in a very calm way. Your child doesn't "need" you, because they are most likely completely unconscious, so the pressure is off to provide a constant source of activities and emotional support in the way you have to when they are on the ward. Instead, you build a very close relationship with the nurse assigned to your child, and with the other parents, who all go through a similar period of bewilderment in the first few hours and days.

It's not appropriate to sleep at the side of the bed in the way you can in most children's wards. However, the hospital will allow you to stay, and will do what they can to provide accommodation. At Guys, I slept in staff accommodation, in waiting rooms, on camp beds. in the hospital school classroom alongside 20 or more complete strangers, until several days later when we reached the top of the waiting list for the gold star of hospital parent accommodation – The Ronald McDonald House at Guys.

Ronald McDonald Houses are really wonderful resources, although there are only 14 of them in the UK so far, all attached to major hospitals, and offering a "home from home" for families of seriously ill children. They are beautifully appointed houses, with every possible comfort you could imagine, as well as cooking and laundry facilities, luxurious bathrooms, and a lovely team of staff to support families in our situation.

We were allocated an enormous room, with a bed for Francesca and a cot for Adam who was only a couple of months old at the time. For the first time in Toby's hospital career, our whole family could be together while I supported Toby.

At the Guy's Ronald McDonald house, there was room to accommodate 16 families, and the friendships and support we received from other families who were going through the same awful times as we were made a huge difference and some remain lifelong friends.

Back to intensive care. Despite the monitors and machines, and the intensive nursing care, once I got used to the environment it was surprising how calmly and slowly things seemed to happen. I think I expected dramatic events to be unfolding all the time, and although they did happen sometimes, they were rare. The level of management and control that the machinery is able to deliver in keeping lungs breathing and hearts beating and blood flowing means that, in the majority of cases, even the most severely ill patients remain relatively stable.

When the worst that can happen does

Sadly, that doesn't mean that everyone makes a complete recovery. The medical technology that exists now means it is often possible to prolong life indefinitely, but sometimes the medical team and the families have to make very difficult decisions about withdrawing treatment, turning the machines off, and precipitating the end of a life. Any death is a tragedy, but I just don't have the words to convey the profoundly raw heartbreak that hangs in the air when such decisions have to be taken about a child.

Although it can sometimes happen, it is rare that death on an intensive care unit is dramatically sudden and unexpected. The hospital drama scenario with dozens of doctors fighting to keep people alive is something I have only seen once in intensive care, although maybe I've just been very lucky.

What normally happens is that, despite every possible intervention and treatment, the child is not responding, and the constant monitoring of their vital signs shows no improvement or even indicates a deterioration. There comes a point when the medical team must make a decision to withdraw treatment, allowing the natural process of death to occur.

There will probably have been a number of discussions with the parents by this time, and the doctors endeavour to be as sensitive as possible, but there really isn't a perfect way to tell a parent that there is no hope for their child. Often, doctors will try and enlist the parent's involvement in these difficult decisions, and while that may help parents feel more in control and therefore more able to accept what is happening, it can sometimes seem to parents like they are being asked to make a life and death decision about their own child, and they can be left with the unthinkable feeling that they have somehow been complicit in the sanctioning of their own child's death.

These are obviously very difficult conversations for doctors to initiate. The team of doctors working in any paediatric intensive care unit are among the most committed, technically competent and caring individuals within the medical profession. They chose this branch of medicine so that they can to use their skills and training to save lives at the very cutting edge of medical technology, and no matter how often they have had to do it, telling parents that their child is going to die is the hardest part of their job, and can affect them deeply too.

Sometimes they strive to be so sensitive, though, that if this wasn't such a heartbreaking subject, there would be a rich vein of black humour running through some of their botched attempts to communicate the facts. Once, a doctor told me "Well, I assume you always imagined that this coming winter would be a difficult one for all of you. I think that winter may be coming tonight". Then he reached out, squeezed my hand, and almost ran from the bedside.

I didn't have a clue what I had just been told. I thought he had just paraphrased a King Lear quote. A nurse later had to translate – Toby wasn't expected to still be alive in the morning.

Once the very difficult decision is taken that there are no options left for a child, things are generally handled very sensitively indeed. In nearly all of these situations whenever possible, the child is moved to a side room to allow more privacy for the parents and family members.

There are often some very difficult conversations to have about organ donation. It may be something that most parents haven't even given a moment's thought to before, and now, at the most emotionally-charged time of their entire lives, there are decisions to be made over this very difficult and emotive subject.

Parents may get a visit from the hospital's organ donation team, who are very skilled at leading these difficult conversations in the most sensitive way possible.

If you ever find yourself in this awful situation, please don't feel that there is a "right" thing to do. The only right thing to do is to do what feels right to you and the very closest members of your immediate family.

For some families, knowing that their child's organs live on and give fresh hope to someone else is a source of immense comfort. Other families feel that their child has had to cope with far too much already, and that the efforts to save their life has left their body already battered and bruised, and they simply want their child's body left alone in peace with no further invasive procedures. Some families can accept certain organs being used for donation but not others. Every family is unique, with their own set of values, beliefs and experiences, and there are probably as many viewpoints on organ donation as there are families.

Whatever your feelings, trust them, and go with them. The only right thing to do is whatever will not add extra pain to an already devastating set of circumstances.

There should also be a bereavement team on hand to help you through these difficult last few hours of your child's life, and to be there for you in the coming weeks.

The medical team will often encourage parents to help them decide when would be best to start withdrawing treatment so that their child can have as peaceful and natural a death as possible. It is often left for several hours or even until a day or so later, before the ventilator will be disconnected. Things may seem like they have slowed down to almost slow-motion during this period, and there will be plenty of time to talk through a lot of very pressing issues with the relevant people if parents need to do so. There should be time for other relatives to come and say their goodbyes, to spend time with the child, comforting and stroking them or talking or singing to them.

The staff will do everything in their power to support parents and their wishes in any way they can, and to answer any of their questions or to talk through what is likely to happen once the ventilator and other equipment is withdrawn. I know some parents who have successfully negotiated that they take their child home so that they can die in their own surroundings, which was exactly the right thing to do for them. Other times, a family may choose to transfer their child to a hospice. However, moving a terminally ill child is not always possible, or the right thing to do.

It is likely that, by this stage, parents have become very close to some of the members of the PICU team by now, and they are accustomed to the environment so that it no longer seems clinical and sterile, but has almost become a second home. Moving a child back home would mean that they would be supported by a local palliative care team whom the parents don't know, when the whole family might be better supported by a team they already know and trust. Additionally, the move home could create extra trauma for the child, and their condition might deteriorate during the transfer.

However, if you are in this situation, and you feel you would prefer to bring your child back home, it is important that you discuss this with the team and explore the options.

One very comforting aspect of this period is that there is no longer the intensity of treatment, and your child will not be subjected to any more painful, traumatic and invasive procedures.

Another very important point to consider is who else you want to be present when your child dies. Many parents, at the time when they are feeling very vulnerable, and at their least assertive, feel pressurised by other family members who want to be present.

This is a whole area which is hardly ever discussed, so there are no accepted norms of social behaviour in these matters whatsoever. However, there is a sort of cultural iconic scenario probably manufactured by Hollywood that the whole extended family is packed around the bedside weeping and wailing in unison, and saying the most beautifully poignant and carefully chosen few words. Unfortunately, this is seldom the reality.

Instead, I have often seen bereft parents having extra stress piled on them by their relatives who are trying to pull rank and prove their own sense of importance by trying to insist that they must be there for the child's last breath. You may be incredibly close to your own parents, but still want those last precious few moments with your child alone. You may absolutely loathe one sister-in-law while another is your best friend – so on top of everything else you are finding yourself working through a minefield of tact and diplomacy and trying to deflect squabbles as to who has the "right" to be at the bedside and who hasn't. You really don't need the two sets of grandparents scoring points and indulging in one-upmanship by the bedside, if the people concerned have never before been able to behave with any civility towards each other

This is one of those moments that is far too important to allow other people's sensitivity and egos to dictate to you. If you don't feel strong enough to communicate your feelings, ask one of the nurses to talk to your relatives. Apart from anything else, your family are less likely to argue with a member of staff.

There are halfway measures too: maybe you want to be there with your child on your own or with your partner, yet your parents are so understandably concerned about you that they want to be there to offer you their love and support. Perhaps you can agree that they are present in the hospital building, but not in the room itself.

Another very important issue to decide is how to prepare your other children for what is happening, and how to best support them. Maybe this is where the grandparents can play an important role, and take the siblings under their wings. What about photos? Some parents later take huge comfort from the last photos of the siblings together at the bedside; if your other children are very small, a photo like this could be very helpful when they are older, and want to know more about the sibling they may barely remember.

To lose a sibling is something that stays with a child forever, it becomes part of their history, a piece of the fabric of their sense of self. How children are involved or excluded from these difficult times will also have a huge impact on their ability to grieve appropriately. It really is worth talking to the bereavement team about how best to support your other children during these awful times, and of course, a lot depends on the age of the child and their level of understanding, too.

When a child dies, it feels like time has stopped still. There is usually a very tranquil atmosphere, and everyone will have pulled together to ensure that death is both peaceful and calm. It may have been some time since you were last able to hold your child close, and some parents take great comfort from the fact that their child is no longer attached to so much machinery, and no longer has all the invasive leads and lines invading their little bodies. Many parents continue to hold their child in their arms for quite a considerable time after they have died, this can seem like the absolute right and natural thing to do.

Eventually, your child's body will be moved to the mortuary, but you can go with them too. Some parents choose to carry their child, wrapped in blankets, to the mortuary themselves, and this has been a source of comfort for some of my friends many years later. Teddy bears, too, are always welcome in the mortuary.

This has been an exceptionally difficult topic to write about, and I'm sure it hasn't been easy for you to read about either. Hopefully this is something that will never, ever happen to you or anybody you hold dear. Sadly, however, it can and does happen, and disabled children so often have other medical conditions that can develop complications, that sometimes it feels that death is never far away. I lived with this reality every day for 10 years and I never dared hope that Toby would still be with us into early adulthood.

In our society, losing a child is so fortunately a rare event, that we don't have an accepted culture of child death anymore. For parents who have to face what is every parent's worst fear, there is very little information in the public domain as to what will happen, what to expect, and how to cope. It is also a very isolating experience, and one that other people may feel completely hopeless about knowing what to say or do to reach out and offer comfort and friendship.

When Toby was little and we knew that he was unlikely to survive, often thoughts of his death would fill my head, and it was awful. However, looking back, while I don't think for a moment these uninvited thoughts would have alleviated the awfulness had it really happened, these thoughts may have helped in some ways.

At least I was very prepared and clear about some of the related issues, like who would be present at the end, how I felt about organ donation, and how I would best support Francesca and Adam if and when the worst might happen.

I will never forget how it felt to come so close to losing Toby, not just once but time and time again. I don't think I've ever been able to take anything totally for granted ever since. One thing that will never change though, is my eternal sense of gratitude and good fortune that Toby is still with us, a huge and integral part of our family, and now healthy enough to have a real chance of a future spanning many decades to come.

SOME ADVICE

Look after yourself. In PICU your child should be being cared for expertly, and you will need your strength when this period comes to an end. Now is the time to pace yourself, ensure you're getting enough sleep and that you're eating properly.

Nothing can prepare you for seeing your own child so desperately ill. Just go with the flow and take every hour as it comes.

When your child is in PICU, you are generally not needed 24/7 at the bedside. This is your chance to try and look after yourself, and to also make time for your other children too, even if it just means that a relative can bring them to meet you in the hospital canteen for long enough to share a hug and an ice-cream.

No matter how young your other children are, they will have picked up that something is very wrong, and they may be frightened and bewildered. I know how hard it is to do, but it will help them if you can explain, in an age-appropriate way, what is happening and why. If their brother or sister doesn't recover, their death will be something that their siblings will carry with them forever. It can help them in the subsequent grieving process if they feel they have been included, have had a chance to explore their own feelings with a trusted adult, and they have been able to prepare for what may happen. This may include an opportunity to say their own goodbye to their sibling.

Think through and mentally prepare if you are able to, about your wishes should your child not recover. If the worst happens, it can help if you and your partner are already clear in your own minds about other family members being present or not, how to explain things to your children, and what you feel about organ donation. It may make these things easier to cope with if you have done some preliminary thinking around the issues already.

Every intensive care unit has its own rules on visitors; it may be that children are not allowed to visit, even brothers and sisters of the ill child. So you may have to arrange urgent childcare for your other children. Don't be afraid to ask for help from your friends and family – you may be surprised at how times like this bring out the very best in the people you know, who will want to do all they can to help.

CHAPTER 12
CAMHS

Depending on your child's diagnosis, behaviour and social development, at one stage or another you may find that you encounter CAMHS, which stands for Child and Adolescent Mental Health Service.

They tend to operate within local Borough boundaries, and each local CAMHS seems to offer a slightly different type of service, and if your local CAMHS doesn't offer the type of service that your child would benefit from, then there really isn't anything much you can do about it.

Every CAMHS is massively overstretched, and aims to see all children with Mental Health issues. Even getting on their waiting list can seem like you have to jump through a load of hoops first, and when you have gained a golden ticket of a waiting list place, it's not uncommon to then have to wait several months to be seen. However, they will fast-track emergencies, so children who are at severe risk are usually seen within a couple of days.

Generally, you need to be referred to CAMHS by your GP, although in certain circumstances, these referrals can come from the local Social Services or the Education departments. However, even getting a referral is hard, and whatever the presenting problem it must be significant enough to merit a referral in the first place.

If it's a behaviour problem, by the time you get to the front of the queue the behaviour may be totally established and have also worsened considerably. During adolescence, many disabled youngsters become incredibly frustrated and angry at exactly the same time that they are often growing taller, stronger and fitter than their parents. The surge of hormones causes a storm of emotions to flood through every teenager, but when that teenager also has disabilities to contend with, these emotions can magnify situations that otherwise would be reasonably easy to handle. The outbursts and upsets that once were relatively manageable can now escalate into a much more serious problem. When these older children become angry they can lash out violently, or destroy property, and it doesn't take very long at all before family life becomes intolerable.

There are also many disabled youngsters who are displaying sexual problems too. The onset of adolescence can be a very frightening time, and there are new feelings and sensations to understand and to cope with. Appropriateness of behaviour can become a very difficult issue for many teenagers with disabilities, and this, too, can lead to a whole new set of problems for the child and their family.

Teenagers become much more acutely aware of their body-image, and their ability to fit in and conform to the social norms of their peer-group. For teenagers with disabilities, this can be an especially difficult time. They have to face an acutely painful realisation that normality is something they will never be able to achieve, and this can herald the onset of all manner of mental health issues, from eating disorders, self-harm through to suicidal thoughts and tendencies.

It is not unusual to be left with little or no support for six months or more before you can see a specialist at CAMHS. The waiting times vary considerably from one area to another. Meanwhile parents have nowhere to turn and no knowledge base to understand how to manage or counter these problems. The child themselves doesn't necessarily understand that what they are doing is wrong, or dangerous, or that there could be very serious consequences. All they are experiencing is a bewilderment of all these new mood swings and hormones racing around their bodies and they can become frightened and depressed and very angry.

When Toby was 13, he suddenly started having violent and aggressive outbursts, and there have been some seriously terrifying moments in our house. I have learnt lots of different strategies and I am a thousand times better at managing his behaviour than I once was, but it took a very long time, real determination and several major struggles before I was able to access specialist services to help me understand how best to manage his outbursts.

During that time, I have heard the same phrase over and over again, "All behaviour is a form of communication". When our children don't have coherent or fluent speech, sometimes the only way they have of telling us how much they are hurting inside is to lash out or smash things up. Understanding this phrase has helped me see things much more from Toby's perspective, which is essential if we, as parents, are to get alongside our children and be able to help them through these very difficult years.

By the time parents get to see a specialist at CAMHS, they are often desperate for help, and this is where so often things get a heck of a lot worse before they get better. The simple fact is that CAMHS isn't sufficiently resourced to be able to offer the specialist, long-term help that families like ours so badly need.

Consequently, there are a fair number of parents who are extremely disappointed with the lack of help they are able to access for their child. The basic, sad fact is that paediatric mental health services in the UK simply are nowhere near adequately resourced to be able to help all the children that so badly need specialist intervention.

Largely, parents often have to find ways to help their child themselves, either by accessing charities specialising in their child's difficulty, which may run workshops or self-help groups, or by researching and reading up on the problem themselves, or by employing a private therapist.

If you find yourself in this situation, try and talk it through with other parents in your circle, talk to your child's school as well as your local social services to see if anyone knows of any services that exist outside of CAMHS, which may be able to offer help and support to both you and your child.

There are at least 3 important things that CAMHS can offer. Firstly, an assessment and a diagnosis. At least then you know what you are dealing with. Secondly they can offer a range of drugs that may control behaviour, or calm the child down, or anti-depressants if the diagnosis includes an element of depression either as the main presenting diagnosis or a secondary one. In some cases this can work extremely well, but it doesn't in every case, and wasn't appropriate at all with Toby. Many parents have reservations about medication that controls behaviour and mood. If this is the case with you, discuss all your concerns with the CAMHS Team, they are very informative, and they generally won't prescribe anything unless it has a good chance of helping. Thirdly, CAMHS can support you in accessing other services that may help your child, for instance with educational statementing or gaining a place in a more appropriate school setting.

Through CAMHS Toby was offered Music Therapy. It worked really well for him, and he came to love his early Monday morning sessions. It took several months, but slowly he began to emerge from his own world and understand that he had the power and ability to reach out and communicate, not always necessarily with words, but with a whole range of things. For us, Music Therapy was a breakthrough, and it was like watching a penny dropping or a light-bulb moment deep within Toby as he learned that if he made certain of his needs known, his circle of trusted adults would try and meet those needs.

For Toby, then and now, the main trigger for his behaviour outbursts is the breakdown of his video equipment. You would honestly think someone had cut both his legs off, such is his level of distress when he can't watch his pre-school TV episodes easily.

We would get into this hopeless spiral of behaviour where he would have fiddled with the back of his video player and pulled the scart lead out, so the TV wouldn't play his videos. So he would start screaming and throwing videos as missiles at whoever tried to help him. While you bent down to reinsert the scart lead, he would be pulling hair, hitting, kicking, and keeping a steady pace of video missiles aimed at your head. In short, you had a simple choice; either fix the scart lead but risk very serious injury, or sit with him and try and restrain his lashing out, and also risk a serious injury. Unless there was another very brave adult in the house, so we could both fix the equipment and keep him from attacking at the same time, we would be stuck in this no-win situation for hours on end.

Over time, the music therapy taught him patience. Not much patience at first, maybe 5 or 10 seconds, but it was such a breakthrough. Music therapy taught him that it was OK, he could trust us, and we wanted to help him. He's still not brilliant at it, but compared to where he once was, these problems are easy-peasy now. If his devices stop working, we now get a theatrical "OH NO" from him, followed by "MUMMY" and "BROKEN" and he'll hand it to me to fix. OK so I have to fix it in about 25 seconds or things might get a bit tricky, but it's all so much easier than it used to be.

We also eventually managed to access a specialist behavioural service by persuading our local CAMHS to refer us to a neighbouring CAMHS, which offered a dedicated learning disability service.

No one ever tells you that these services even exist, and then they move heaven and earth to prevent you accessing such services. Bottom line and it all comes down to money, but the ironic thing is that, had Toby's frustration not been significantly lessened, the taxpayer would have had to eventually pay for a care facility with the specialisms to deal with such extreme behaviour throughout his entire life. Such facilities are not cheap, the overall cost would have run into several hundreds of thousands of extra pounds over the 40 or 50 more years that Toby is now predicted to have in front of him. That is just looking at the problem in stark financial terms. Of much greater concern to me is that Toby would have had to look forward to a life of being locked away in a high security residential care centre, unable to access all the things he really loves about life, and probably miles away. Perhaps somewhere like Winterbourne View, where horrific abuse was meted out to young people just like Toby.

It was this specialist CAMHS service that really made a huge difference. Again not immediately, and it took a lot of really intensive work on my part too, but we eventually got to a place that is mostly manageable.

There was a very highly trained specialist nurse who came to visit us every week for over a year. He devised forms for me to fill out, so we could pin down exactly the frequency, severity and form that each outburst took, and he got to know Toby and the sorts of things that motivated him. Essentially, I think this specialist nurse had to work far harder on me than he did on Toby, and I don't think I was the easiest parent to work with. At times I was pretty stubborn and resistant about a lot of the changes that had to be made. The thing is though, in the end I was persuaded, simply because I began to see that it works.

Basically, I had to learn the hard way that the only way to change Toby's behaviour was to make fairly significant changes in the way I responded to him. Over time, and with lots of big issues broken down into tiny little steps, his behaviour changed too. Things aren't perfect and probably never will be, but with all that Toby has had to contend with during his very difficult start in life and the unfairness of his profound disabilities, we can allow him the odd little outburst. I now know that I can usually reach out to him and help him resolve the pain he's feeling, and he trusts me enough to let me do it.

CAMHS also eventually diagnosed Toby with severe autism. It's only a tiny part of who Toby is and his whole condition is much more complex than that, but I had suspected he also had autism since he was a toddler. It's interesting that now, in addition to all his other weird and wonderful diagnoses, having autism as well makes him seem as if he is more mainstream-disabled, it's a diagnosis that most people understand, and in a funny way, it has opened doors to him that were closed before. Certainly, having Autism elicits a better level of understanding from people, and that has benefitted him greatly.

Even though he is clearly autistic, Toby loves people. He is charismatic, funny, engaging, cheeky, mischievious and very loving. All characteristics not normally associated with autism at all, but it makes him very easy to love, not just by his devoted family, but by virtually everyone he comes into contact with.

CAMHS is responsible for all children with any form of mental health problem, and the vast majority of children they see are mainstream children who are exhibiting a whole range of very acute mental health symptoms. CAHMS is the source of emotional support to mainstream suicidal teenagers, those who self-harm or who have extreme eating disorders, those who are having school issues, as well as any child displaying a whole range of anti-social or depressive behaviours or any child who is severely troubled in any way. In our 21st century society, you can imagine how overstretched they are already, without having to factor in the range of problems our lovely children can also exhibit.

Many parents are extremely worried that their child isn't quite fitting in, or isn't quite communicating as easily as their peers, and begin to wonder if their child might be autistic. Generally, it is also only CAMHS who can make such a diagnosis, so at any given time there are many families with children of all ages waiting for their child to be seen in the belief that their autism fears are likely to be confirmed with a formal diagnosis of ASD, or Autistic Spectrum Disorder.

These parents often hold out real hope that not only will their child be diagnosed, but that CAMHS can also give both parents and child tools to help them minimise the effects of autism. It really isn't that straightforward at all. Often children are really difficult for CAMHS to assess properly, because generally speaking, children and especially teenagers, and doubly especially if they are autistic, simply don't always easily engage with the adults working at CAMHS. It can be a long, laborious and often extremely difficult process to reach a diagnosis with any degree of certainty.

In most cases that do eventually go on to receive an autism diagnosis, parents then are shocked and bewildered to find that they often may not be offered any other support or help whatsoever. There is a belief that CAHMS staff, being the experts, will somehow help them control their child's behaviour, but most CAHMS teams simply don't have the expertise, the funding or the manpower to be able to offer anything along these lines.

There are places you can go, support organisations you can join, and books you can read, but essentially for most parents, they have to learn the strategies all by themselves, digging deep into their own resources to find an acceptable way forward.

Unfortunately, this is a recurrent theme with every aspect of disability. It often boils down to parents like us being resilient, persistent and determined enough to solve many of our own problems.

TIPS, TRICKS AND STRATEGIES

All the same ones from Chapter 10, plus....

Don't expect too much.

Be prepared to be creative in finding solutions for your child's difficulties, since the service you really need may not exist at your local CAMHS.

If you have months to wait, read everything you can on your child's symptoms, and start to see if you can implement strategies while you're waiting.

CHAPTER 13
Education

Every parent wants two basic things from the education system for their children; to do well and to be happy. Why is that often so much to ask for just because your child has a disability?

There are far too many disabled children who are completely and needlessly failed by the education system, either because they have been unable to reach their full academic potential or because they have been damaged psychologically by the whole school system, or in many cases, both.

Why is this the case, and how can you make things better for your child?

There are so many different factors converging at the interface of education and disability. The most obvious ones are the type of school – mainstream or special school. Many parents also experience a huge difference in provision and resources between primary and secondary school. The experience of pupils is influenced by the type of disability a child has and its severity. Additionally, your child's educational experience will be affected by whether they are "statemented" or not.

We can look at each of these points in turn, although I won't go into great detail about the current statementing system, simply because the legislation is in the process of being completely overhauled, so there will be some significant changes to how the whole special needs education system is administered in the next couple of years. However, these changes will be implemented by the same people who are delivering education to children like ours across the country, and what we really need to see happening is an attitude shift in many of these people's thinking.

Statement of Special Educational Needs/ Education Health and Care Plan (EHCP)

A Statement of Special Educational Needs is a legally-binding document that is prepared individually for a disabled child, and sets out in detail the extra help, resources and adjustments that must be made by the school to give that child the best chance of fulfilling their educational potential. It is soon going to be replaced by a new document covering not just educational needs, but also Health and Social Care too. Both documents are based on a number of separate assessments of the child, and can take 6 months to finish. One encouraging aspect to this new document is that they will be quicker to prepare – the current limit of 26 weeks has been reduced to 20.

Statements are a source of tremendous stress and anxiety to parents. Getting one in the first place is like pulling teeth but not quite as much fun, and there are conflicting interests right from the start. A child with a statement will need extra funding from the local authority, so from a parent's perspective, it often seems as though the local authority is dragging its feet and putting every obstacle in the way of attaining one, to save money. Then every year, the statement needs to be reviewed to take into account the changing needs of the growing child, again, something parents find adds totally unnecessary stress to their already overstretched life.

So although there are some pretty major changes going on, the staff administering the process and the funding issues will remain pretty much the same, so I can't see that the parental experience of the process is going to greatly improve.

One major drawback of this system, the Statement or the EHCP, is that not every child who has special educational needs will get one. This is very much a tiered system, and the Statement or EHCP is a bit like getting the first prize. Unless your child's disability is very obvious indeed, you will have to use every ounce of battle in your body to get one, and even then you still might not achieve it.

There are two other tiers to this system currently, called School Action and School Action Plus, which acknowledges that your child needs extra help, but neither tier carry the same level of clout as the Statement does. As the new system is overhauled, School Action and School Action Plus are going to be merged together, and it is expected that many children currently catered for by these tiers will be excluded by the new criteria.

Every school has a SENCO, which stands for Special Educational Needs Co-ordinator, who is a senior teacher with responsibility for the implementation of all of these documents as well as the well-being of all disabled pupils. It is the SENCOs who also administer and implement the School Action and School Action Plus documents, the difference between them being that in School Action all extra help is provided internally by the school, whereas School Action Plus also has the involvement of external specialists, such as an occupational therapist or a speech and language therapist.

Both Francesca and Adam were denied access to the statementing process, but they both were assigned to School Action Plus, yet despite this they were both let down very badly by the whole school experience, both educationally and psychologically. Toby, of course, was statemented very early on, but his disabilities are so severe that the need was very obvious.

To gain acceptance to any special school a Statement is currently a preliminary requirement, so unless your child is awarded a statement before they are of compulsory school age, your first step is to talk to the SENCO at your child's mainstream school. This initial discussion can be initiated either by the parent or by the SENCO, depending on who first wishes to raise concerns with the other.

The next step is for the SENCO to arrange for the educational psychologist to meet with your child, and to do an initial assessment, either formally or informally. This is the first stumbling block. Although every school has an assigned educational pyschologist (EP), the amount of EP time that is allocated to each school is dependant on the perceived need of the cohort of pupils within the individual school.

Francesca was already 9 years old when she was diagnosed with Tourette's Syndrome, and suddenly a lot of the school issues she had struggled with began to make sense. So I made an appointment to see the SENCO within a couple of days. Although sympathetic to the situation, the SENCO explained that because that primary school was perceived to have a socio-economic cohort of low need, the school was only allocated enough EP time to see at most a couple of pupils a term. If Francesca was to go onto the waiting list, it would take at least 2 years before she could see an EP, and she would already be in High School by then. She also told me that because Francesca was so bright and presented so well she would almost certainly not be eligible for a Statement,

We couldn't afford to wait that long, because decisions concerning High School choices would have to be made in just over a year from then, and I wanted to have some idea of her educational need before selecting the most appropriate high school.

So we had to go down the route of employing a private EP ourselves. The report was fascinating. Francesca was performing in reading and maths at the levels expected of a 17 year old and a 15 year old respectively at the tender age of 9, which was quite remarkable, particularly when an attainment of a 17 year old was the highest score possible on this particular test. However, it also made some very insightful comments about aspects of learning that Francesca was going to struggle with as she got older and school became more formal. It made some very clear recommendations of steps that should be taken immediately to prevent real problems further down the line.

I took the report into school, and Francesca was put onto School Action Plus. I pointed out the recommendations, but they weren't really taken on board because school felt that Francesca couldn't really need them because she was functioning educationally at such a high level, and was already a star pupil in many respects.

We have the 11 Plus system in our area, which means that some of our local High Schools are called Grammar Schools, and select their pupils solely on the basis of their academic potential. Francesca walked the entrance exam. For several months I was an incredibly proud parent. However, as soon as she started secondary school it all went horribly, disastrously wrong. The teachers at this elite school just didn't "get" special needs or disability. They had no clue about what the term "making reasonable adjustments" meant. She started getting detention after detention for things that she just couldn't help. I watched her mental state deteriorate. I watched as she was bullied, not by the pupils but by the teaching staff. I joined the Governing Body to support the school and maybe to be able to influence their attitudes from the inside. We had meeting after meeting at school about her, each time they interpreted her disabilities as being naughty and unengaged, and added sanction after sanction. She was a nervous wreck.

Eventually the school agreed to bring in another educational psychologist to do a further assessment on Francesca. This EP was great, and wrote a very long and detailed report, making 10 very clear and easily implemented recommendations, all of which were low-cost or no-cost solutions. A meeting was called with the SENCO, the Head Teacher, Francesca, myself and the EP, plus a few others, and the 10 recommendations were discussed and explained fully. You could tell around that table that the staff thought this was all a fuss over nothing, and the upshot was that not one of the recommendations was implemented, and Francesca continued to face derision and humiliation from many members of the teaching staff.

Francesca kept begging not to have to go to school, but of course I made her go in every day.

One day, after school, I received phone calls from parents of girls in her class, parents I didn't even know, all calling independently of each other. Each of them told me about a very unpleasant encounter Francesca had had that day with teaching staff. What I was hearing was truly shocking, and these parents were also telling me their own daughters were extremely distressed by what they had witnessed. I realised then that bullying isn't something that is only carried out by other pupils, this was by the teaching staff, adults who were charged with keeping my daughter safe both physically and emotionally. The incident was sufficiently serious to make me realise that enough was enough. I didn't know how I was going to pull it off, but I knew that day that we had reached the end of the line, Francesca had already had to cope with too much, and she was never ever going to go back to that school.

The school had nearly broken her. She was on the verge of a nervous breakdown, and I am still so grateful to those parents for alerting me to understanding the severity of what Francesca had been facing on a daily basis. I had known things were bad, but I had trusted the very well-respected school to eventually sort things out, and, like a lot of parents, I had put some of the difficulties down to adolescence and teenagers being a bit difficult.

It was three years before she was strong enough to return to education. She was accepted by a special education unit locally that only takes on pupils who are not mentally well enough to go to mainstream schools. She joined them in Year 11, less than a year before she was due to sit GCSE's. Coming back to education after having missed three full years of school, I expected that there would be a significant amount of catching up to do, but there wasn't, because finally she was being supported in the way that was right for her. The following summer, just 8 months later and against all the odds, she passed 11 GCSEs with very good grades, and was also well on her way back to being the happy, chatty and delightfully engaging Francesca that the grammar school experience had all but destroyed.

We had a similar experience 4 years later with Adam and his mainstream comprehensive. He too, is very bright, but was unable to access education in the same way as his peers. The first I knew of any real difficulty whatsoever was when I found him after a failed suicide attempt. We are still working through the reverberations of that one three years later, but at least I knew of the existence of this great little special education unit, and he was accepted a few months later.

His school, another highly respected local high school, also took a very unsympathetic approach towards his difficulties. Yet again, they looked at our family circumstances, yet again they apportioned blame to my parenting skills in the light of the difficulties both Francesca and Toby had. They acted as if I had given them a gift, a "get-out-of-jail-free" card, a perfect excuse to let themselves entirely off the hook for the fact that Adam had nearly died because they had failed him. They looked at us, and very clearly came to the conclusion that we were a dysfunctional family, and that I was fairly and squarely to blame.

We had meeting after meeting, and it became very apparent that Adam wasn't the main focus of these at all, the only thing that mattered was potential reputational damage to the school, and that the easiest way to prevent that was to discredit me as much as possible. The meeting minutes were doctored to place the staff in a better light every time, whilst every attempt was made to undermine my contribution and my credibility.

It is just too easy for these people to lay the blame on our family environment. After all, his brother Toby was profoundly disabled and his sister had fallen by the wayside, educationally, too. They projected the view that I was clearly not coping, and therefore had neglected my parenting duties and it was me that had failed Adam.

The most shocking aspect of this is that, even if we had been dysfunctional, surely they have a legal duty of care towards every child, and a moral obligation to protect the most vulnerable children who may come from less than perfect family backgrounds? I am articulate, experienced in meetings, and I was always well supported by a trusted ally who accompanied me each and every time, yet I struggled and failed to be heard, understood and taken seriously.

Francesca and Adam both had serious diagnosed conditions, they were both on School Action Plus, and they both had Educational Psychology reports that made a number of easy to implement recommendations. Yet because they were both extremely bright academically, and they were both polite, well-mannered kids who presented well, their respective schools chose to ignore the recommendations and in so doing lit the touch-paper that caused them both to free-fall into severe mental health difficulties for most of their teenage years. One school chose to blame Francesca and punished her for her disabilities, the other chose to blame me for my apparent poor parenting skills. Of course, the schools still believe that they knew best.

Toby's experience, thankfully, was very different. He had a statement and attended excellent special schools throughout. In contrast, we never had a moment's worry with him, he always loved school and he made tremendous progress year on year in his own limited fashion. Staff at special schools generally have a completely different, and much more positive, attitude towards parents. They understand that most of us are doing the absolute best job we can to support our children. It always felt as if we were all on the same side, and it makes everything so much easier when there is that level of trust. I built up superb relationships with Toby's school staff, and some are very good friends outside of the school environment.

Best of all, the children themselves are the real winners when they feel that all the adults, both at home and at school, are working together as a strong team.

One of the hardest things a parent can face is seeing their child having a miserable, desolate time at school. Every parent wants their child to do well academically and socially, and for your child not to be coping is very difficult to handle. Parents themselves can become very emotional too, and it can affect the whole family. School is compulsory, and most parents don't know what their options are, or even if they have any options. It's also very difficult to know where to go to get the support you need, it's often the case that there are no other families in your circle that have faced these difficulties.

The day I took the decision that Francesca was never going to go back to school, I simply didn't know how I was going to pull it off. Deliberately keeping a child off school went so deeply against everything I held dear and believed in, and it is generally regarded within our society as a profoundly irresponsible thing to do. I knew parents had gone to prison for keeping their children away from school, and everyone I tried to talk it over with was shocked and horrified that I was even considering such a thing, but I knew that going in to school again was entirely the wrong thing for Francesca.

Education is important, but so is mental health, self-esteem and self-confidence. Any child who is miserable at school will not be able to learn effectively and will fall behind, making their situation even worse, because they will be getting disapproval from their teachers and feeling that they are less able than their peers. Every year, a small number of children commit suicide because school-life is so intolerable, and a much larger number of children are suffering irreparable psychological damage that will have a life-long effect. There must be an even greater number of children who are desperately unhappy. Given a straight choice between education and mental well-being, I believe that mental well-being is of paramount importance. Your child can catch up on their education, but may never recover from the psychological effects of having a really painful school experience.

There are no easy options, but there are options, and you will have to be prepared to be very firm and stick to your guns in backing your child. School is generally regarded as being compulsory but it is not. It is education that is compulsory. This means that you can keep your child at home as long as you can prove that they are gaining an education, otherwise known as Home Schooling.

This is a viable option, and one that many families in these circumstances pursue every year. You have to write a letter detailing your intentions to both your child's school and your local authority, and you will have educational inspections every now and again to check on the type of education being provided. Some parents use this option to buy some time, and to help their child recover and regain their confidence, before applying to another school a few months later.

Another option is the medical route. This means seeing your GP, explaining that your child is depressed, and asking for them to be signed off from school, with a referral to CAHMS. Many GPs are reluctant to encourage what they see as school non-attendance, and you may need to return many times and to make a really strong case before a GP may be persuaded to provide a medical certificate.

You can talk to your child's school, and see if they would be willing to provide school-work for your child to complete at home. The response you are likely to get is variable. Some schools will be very reluctant to admit that a child in their care is unable to attend school. They may see it as an indictment on their reputation, and many parents find teaching staff in these situations to be very unsupportive, and some have felt under extreme pressure to force their child to return to school.

Every local authority has a team of educational welfare officers, the team that used to be known as the truancy officers. Their role is to ensure children are in education, and they can bring legal proceedings against parents who do not comply. However, they can also be very sympathetic in cases like these, and a phone-call to them in the very early days of non-attendance can elicit a helpful and positive response.

We were lucky in that our local authority has a Pupil Referral Unit especially for children who are unable to attend mainstream schools due to mental health issues. Both Francesca and Adam eventually attended this unit, and they both benefitted enormously. However, if your local authority has such a unit, it is likely to be the best kept secret there is, simply because these units are generally very small, and simply couldn't cope with the true demand on places if they were better publicised. A CAMHS Psychiatric referral was essential to gain a place at this unit. You may have to ask directly if such a unit exists locally, and if it doesn't, you can ask what alternative arrangements are made for these children.

Mainstream or Special Schools

This is a controversial debate that has now run for decades. In the past, all disabled children, even those with a high intellect, were educated in special schools. Some of these schools were unable to offer a full academic curriculum in a broad range of subjects leading to nationally recognised qualifications, and therefore there were a large number of pupils who were unable to reach their full potential. As these children reached adulthood, many entered the debate and voiced their rightful and very valid concerns that this was wrong and many have campaigned for the inclusion of all disabled children within mainstream schools.

One of the most high-profile of these people is David Blunkett, who later became the Minister of Education in the Labour Government of the late 1990's. He was very open about his thoughts on this matter, and was very pro-inclusion for all. Over the past 2 decades, there has been intermittent media coverage of the issues, with the received wisdom being that generally speaking, all children would be better served in mainstream education. The concept of inclusion has become a highly-debated and emotive topic, and also somewhat of a politicised ideal.

The legal framework during this period has supported this movement; in 1993 all parents, regardless of the level or severity of their child's disability, were given the legal right to choose a mainstream school for their child, and this has been followed up since by the 1995 Disability Discrimination Act which made it illegal for schools or other educational establishments to discriminate against children with disabilities.

Inclusion is a very noble ideal, and in a perfect world it would be what every parent of a child with disabilities aims to achieve for their children. However, we do not live in a perfect world, and inclusion done on the cheap is anything but perfect. It is much cheaper to educate children with disabilities in mainstream schools, so for both Central and Local Governments it is a much more attractive option.

There is often neither the funding nor the goodwill from schools to properly understand how an individual child's disabilities can impact on their learning in very complex ways. Teaching and support staff are not adequately trained in how our children's educational needs are best met, nor do they receive training on the different behaviours our children may present in class. Many schools have a very limited and unimaginative range of tools and ideas on offer for children with disabilities, particularly for those children who do not appear obviously disabled.

As things stand at the moment, too many mainstream schools have not been able to make the necessary adjustments and modifications that would really create a level playing-field for all children, and truly be able to meet the needs of every child with disabilities. Until this happens, we run the risk of these children failing in mainstream, not just educationally, but also in psychological terms.

There are basically three possible options for choosing a school. Your child's disabilities may be so mild that the mainstream, primary or secondary school may be the right choice. Or it may be that, with extra classroom support, some reasonable adaptations, and a lot of goodwill, even a significantly disabled child may do well with their local peer-group at their local mainstream school.

The second option is what is known as a "Base Unit". These are specialist units within an ordinary primary school, where disabled children can be given the extra support they need, whilst still being able to benefit from the social and other opportunities that a mainstream primary school can offer. Many base units offer a very impressive degree of flexibility, with some children joining their mainstream peer-groups for certain lessons and not for others, with individual timetables tailored for each disabled child. In your local area, there may be a handful of schools with base units, each one perhaps catering for a different type of disability, Autism, Mobility Impairment, Hearing or Sight Impairments, etc. This is a very popular option with many parents, because when it is done well, it can offer the very best of both worlds to our children.

There are downsides, as there are to anything. Sometimes schools with base units may not be very local, and that can be difficult if you have other children in other schools, because it's impossible to be at two places at once for the start and end of each day. This can be overcome by applying for school transport for the child attending the base unit, or by applying for places for all your children to attend the base unit school. However, acquiring school transport can be a very hard battle, and there may not always be vacancies for each of your other children.

Thirdly there are several different types of special schools, each catering for a particular type of need. The main categories of special school are: **PMLD (Profound and Multiple Learning Disability), SLD (Severe Learning Disability), MLD (Moderate Learning Disability, EBD (Emotional and Behavioural Disorders), Speech, Language and Communication Schools**, as well as some schools which specialise in Autism, and both Hearing and Vision Impairments.

The vast majority of these schools are State Day Schools, but there are some boarding schools, and some special schools are run privately, although most places will be funded by the child's local authority.

In our case, an SLD special school was the only option for Toby, and within the secondary SLD school he attended there was also a PMLD class, which he was placed in later on. Not only was special education the right choice educationally, and they were able to concentrate more on helping him develop life skills and a general understanding of the world, but also because of his complex medical needs. It is only in special schools where there is the high level of full-time nursing care that Toby needed during the school day.

Parents of very young children with severe learning disabilities often find it hard to accept the idea of their small disabled child being sent to a special school. I'm sure I am not alone in remembering that I cried buckets for weeks on end at the very thought of Toby going somewhere so alien to anything I had ever known. Then I went to visit some of them. Wow. Bright, colourful, happy, creative, supportive; I could not believe how well-resourced these schools were in terms of pupil to staff ratios and equipment. In one afternoon all my prejudices were swept away, and I simply couldn't wait for him to start and to have so much fun.

15 years later, and I can't remember a single day when he didn't want to go to school. I never had a moment of regret, other than about those weeks I had wasted crying all those silly tears.

I believe very strongly that it was absolutely and totally the right thing for Toby, but I know that it might not be the right thing for every child.

What does concern me is that there may be some parents who are so upset by the whole idea of special schooling that they don't even consider it, and instead send their child to a mainstream setting where he or she may never fit in or find the level of acceptance, friendship, confidence and self-esteem that Toby has benefitted from ever since the day he started school.

There are many benefits to a special school education. Toby grew up among children like himself, children who also had severe learning disabilities. He was ordinary there, he wasn't special, and therefore he didn't get any special treatment. He had to follow the same school rules as everyone else, and I think that has been the most normalising aspect of his entire childhood. He was with staff who had made a deliberate decision to work with severely learning disabled children, and his life has been greatly enriched by the commitment and dedication of the staff to ensure that every child was given a very broad-based opportunity to access different experiences.

Had he instead gone to a mainstream school, he would have been very obviously different to his peers and would have stood out like a sore thumb. I think he could have become self-conscious and lacking in confidence as a result. No matter how hard he would have worked, he would always have been at the bottom of the class, and would not have been able to keep up or engage in most of the lessons. The expertise and skill-set of the mainstream staff would not have been anywhere near the specialist, highly trained skills and experience of the dedicated workforce within a special school, who are experts in getting even the most communication-compromised child learning to express themselves in one way or another.

However, had Toby been of normal intellect but with a physical disability, I would be saying completely the opposite. This is why it is wrong to have a single, generic term to describe the complete spectrum of special needs and disability issues.

The type and severity of your child's disabilty

In educational settings, as in most other organisations, the word "Disability" is a one-size-fits-all term, with no acknowledgement that children who are described by this term encompass a whole range of different abilities, needs and diagnoses, and that therefore a mainstream school which has disabled pupils needs to take a multi-focal approach when attempting to meet their range of needs.

Personally, I would like there to be at least four well-defined subsections to be applied to mainstream provision for disabled children, with an acceptance that some children's needs may overlap two or more of these subsections. I see the needs of disabled children as falling reasonably easily into 5 fairly separate sections as I've outlined below. Currently, mainstream schools seem to offer a very limited range of tools to support disabled children, so I've also added a few ideas of what might actually help, some of which are currently offered by many schools but some are not. It's by no means a definitive list of possibilities, but it would be great if schools could start to think a little bit more "outside the box". It really shouldn't be about what each school can easily offer and already has in place, but about each child, and tailoring solutions to meet their specific additional educational needs.

Physically Disabled – the children who would fall solely into this category would be of age-appropriate intelligence.

Equipment: wheelchairs, walking frames, special classroom seating, standing frames, laptops, dictaphones, slanted desks, easy-grip pens and pencils, ipads or other touch-screen devices.

Environmental: wheelchair-accessible doorframes, grab rails on corridors, all lessons timetabled for ground-floor classrooms, a playground area that is accessible and with a reduced risk of accidental injury caused by able-bodied children.

Therapeutic: access to visiting physiotherapists, timetabled hydrotherapy sessions, occupational therapy.

Learning Support with pastoral care: an assigned learning support assistant when needed, and to keep an eye on the overall welfare and socialisation of the child, with specialist training in disability issues.

Learning Disabled

Modified Curriculum: to allow them to learn at their own pace about things that are meaningful for them.

Learning Support Assistance: a designated learning support assistant either all or part of the time, depending on the severity of the disability, who has also received specialist training in disability issues.

Base Unit: a specialist unit for learning disability pupils within the school.

Equipment: laptops, dictaphones, slanted desks, easy grip pens and pencils, ipad or similar touch-screen device.

Therapeutic: Speech and Language Therapies, Music Therapy, Art Therapy, Drama Therapy, Occupational Therapy.

Environmental: sensory room, safe playground.

Autistic Spectrum Disorder

Equipment: laptops, dictaphones, slanted desks, easy grip pens.

Environmental: quiet room, sensory room, timetable modifications to reduce moving around the school.

Therapeutic: Speech and Language Therapy, Music Therapy, Art Therapy, Drama Therapy, Occupational Therapy, Group Social Skills Sessions.

Learning Support Assistant: an assigned learning support assistant either full or part time depending on severity, who has received specialist training on autism.

Base Unit: a specialist unit within some schools, catering specifically for certain disabilities.

Invisible Disabilities

These are the children, like Francesca and Adam, who tend to get their needs completely overlooked, and they have needs which may require an entirely different approach. They will have a range of disabilities such as Obsessive Compulsive Disorder, Sensory Sensitivities, ADHD, Concentration Difficulties, Tourette's Syndrome, Mental Health issues, Dyspraxia, Dyslexia, Dysgraphia, Chronic Health Disorders... the list is endless.

These children need modifications such as being given lesson notes and handouts PRIOR to lessons, so they are not always on catch-up and feeling pressured to keep up if their concentration wanes during a lesson, a different way of assessing their progress other than essay-style written work – some of the children with OCD or other anxieties may be unable to complete written work due to dyslexia, dyspraxia, perfectionist issues or self-esteem difficulties, so a verbal discussion with a teacher to check their understanding of topics may reduce pressure significantly; a "time-out" card so they can leave the room if they feel overwhelmed; seating plans so that these children are away from noise and close to the teacher to enable better understanding.

A valuable part of education for all children is learning self-discipline, particularly around issues such as persistent lateness or poor organisation skills. Most schools apply sanctions such as detentions for this sort of behaviour.

However, many children with invisible disabilities simply don't have the same capacity to be punctual or to organise themselves as their classmates. If a child with OCD has to repeatedly check every aspect of getting ready for school, they will often be late, due to their disability, not because of deliberately being badly behaved. It is the same for children with ADHD – they may lack the concentration to organise their school-bag and complete their homework on time.

Often, it is the children with this type of invisible disability who face multiple detentions and other sanctions for things they simply cannot help. There would be vast media coverage and national outrage if a child with mobility problems was penalised for not being good at running, yet every day, hundreds of children are being punished simply because they have a disability which prevents them from being organised or being on time for school every day.

Children with Sensory Impairments

The fifth category of children are those with either visual and/or hearing impairments. These children can sometimes do extremely well in a mainstream school, but only if they are given the right sort of support tailored to their individual circumstances. It is very easy to assume that, simply by closing our eyes or covering our ears, we understand the losses these children endure, but it is so much more complex than that. It is not as simple as providing braille-enabled keyboards and a trip-hazard free environment for a child who cannot see. It is also about helping that child explore and understand their world in a way that a sighted child can grasp automatically.

A hearing-impaired child is likely to need intensive speech and language therapy, and a general understanding that children who cannot hear properly can become very isolated and lonely, and will miss out on a lot of the subtle cues that the hearing population take for granted.

With both hearing and sight loss, the severity of the impairment and the way it affects individual children varies immensely. Every child needs to be assessed on a case-by-case basis, and the type of help and intervention needs to be sensitively attuned to the individual needs of each child.

There are also some excellent specialist schools catering for both hearing and visual impairments. The staff at these schools have a wealth of experience and expertise. It may be worth contacting these specialist schools for advice about the best teaching resources and methods, even if you choose a mainstream school for your child.

In a mainstream school, there would need to be particular attention given regarding where they sit in class to maximise their learning experience, and their ability to understand what's going on around them.

Some general thoughts

Mainstream schools who are not effectively meeting the educational needs of our children with disabilities are setting up these children to fail, which is going to achieve nothing other than a child whose self-confidence is in their boots. It simply is not good enough.

In our case, I spoke to staff at all levels of seniority in the schools concerned and it was like talking to a brick wall, the injustice of how my children were being treated simply fell on deaf ears. They couldn't grasp why they should have to make allowances; I was told on one occasion that it would be grossly unfair to all the other children at the school if my children received "special treatment". All I wanted was for their help to create an equal, level playing-field where my children would not be discriminated against because of their disabilities, but in each case, the school couldn't, or wouldn't accept it.

There are other issues about Mainstream inclusion that I have deep concerns about. Obviously it is the cheapest option for both local and central Government, but it is neither properly resourced, nor sufficiently funded to give the disabled children the extra help and assistance in education that they truly need and deserve.

There also needs to be a huge re-training programme, implemented as a matter of urgency within mainstream schools. This may begin to help staff to shift their attitudes and begin to embrace the needs and difficulties of their disabled pupils. We urgently need significantly more understanding and clarity than was my experience with both Francesca and Adam.

Habits and cultures take a long time to change, and meanwhile whole generations of disabled youngsters are risking serious mental harm while current attitudes persist. The over-arching impression I formed during the very difficult months of repeated meetings at both the mainstream secondary schools of my experience was that they resented having to deal with children that didn't fit into neat little boxes.

I have concerns about the direction in which schools seem to be moving. There is a definite trend towards a corporate, branded approach in the way schools are marketing themselves. We now have "chains" of schools too, with several towns having their own branch of a particular branded school. Image is becoming king, and this glossy, corporate style of branding prioritises reputation above all else. Where are the children in all of this? Particularly the ones, often the ones like our children, who can't be pigeon-holed and fit this corporate mould?

This is another huge factor that has been over-looked. Within the UK over the last 20 or so years, there has been a revolution in the way education is delivered, particularly at secondary level. The primary focus of schools is now their ranking within exam league tables, and there simply isn't time for the type of pastoral care that I remember with fondness from my secondary school of the seventies, where all the teachers knew me as a person, not just as a name alongside a line of numbered results on a spreadsheet.

In the race for results, we have lost something very precious from the way we educate our teenagers. It's not just pastoral care; there has also been a widespread homogenisation of the way education is delivered, with every lesson now having a learning objective clearly stated at the beginning of the session, and lessons delivered along formal, structured lesson-plan lines.

When we began a lesson in our school-days, we had no clue where the lesson was going to lead or what we were going to learn. Sometimes neither did the teacher! Some of the best lessons that I remember the most were the very ones that went off-topic because someone had asked an obscure question, and thirty pupils and a teacher would together examine every facet of an argument that wasn't even about the school subject matter sometimes, but was full of the wonder of exploration and learning in the most natural of ways, following the curiosity of a group of young people.

Teachers are under so much pressure to teach particular topics within a particular timescale and in a particular way, and it feels like our children are being force-fed facts and stark knowledge in a very efficient and effective manner, but at the expense of learning how to question and wonder. Even more importantly, we have lost the teacher-child relationships where a teacher had time to get to know their pupils, and notice if a child was in need of emotional support.

At exactly the same time that this revolution has been taking place, whereby all achievement is reduced to a tiny tick-box area just large enough to record the percentage score of the latest assignment of each pupil, the very same schools have been expected to open their arms wide and welcome a new cohort of disabled pupils. Disabled children will never neatly fit into any of those tidy little tick-boxes on the bright and shiny spreadsheet, and thank goodness for that.

TIPS, TRICKS AND STRATEGIES

Don't let them fob you off.

Make sure all your child's needs are clearly stated on the Statement or EHCP.

Look out for any narrative that is vague or open to interpretation, and get it changed to specifics.

Don't accept the Statement or EHCP until you are 100% happy with it.

Believe your child if they tell you school is intolerable.

Don't be afraid to take your child out of school. Home educate them if necessary, or get them medically signed off. Your child's self-esteem is far too valuable to allow the wrong school to destroy it, possibly forever. Don't worry too much about their long-term education. If they are desperately unhappy they won't be performing well in school anyway, and education can be caught up with later. You can never bring back a child who has successfully committed suicide. Once they are feeling stronger, you can find them another school with a different attitude.

Take someone with you to every school meeting, preferably someone that both you and your child trusts, too.

Take copious notes.

Check the minutes carefully, and send them back asking for corrections if you don't feel they are a true reflection of the discussion and tone of the actual meeting.

Ensure that your child is being offered appropriate extra help in class.

Do not be intimidated.

Keep an open mind when choosing your child's school, look at every option, special schools, base units and mainstream.

CHAPTER 14
Social Services

Our children will always rely on professional help, and whilst every family in the land has some involvement from the NHS and our educational services for their children, the vast majority of children will never come to the attention of Social Services.

However, Social Services will always be a dominant feature in the lives of families with disabled children. They hold the keys to all sorts of services, and they can support you in a number of different ways which make your life much easier.

It hasn't always been easy to deal with them, there have been times when I have been driven to distraction by them, irritated, outraged, shocked and appalled by them and what they are proposing for my family, but equally there have been times of enormous gratitude when I knew that they really have risen to the challenge to help, and have supported us to avert a crisis exactly when we needed it the most.

Of the three statutory services, I always found Social Services the easiest and the most pleasant to deal with. We had our ups and downs and run-ins, and yes, they often made me seethe at times too, but I always felt that, deep down, they were on the same side. I think they have embraced the idea of working in partnership with parents much better than either the NHS or education have so far, they understand that better outcomes happen when everyone pulls together to support the child.

Whereas the other two services are there primarily for your child's well-being, Social Services, when they work well, will take a "Big Picture" view of the whole family and how your child's disabilities are impacting on everyone. I always felt that they were there for me, and yes, in our situation, Social Services did work well, and our Social Worker backed us all the way.

It's easy enough to accept help from the education and medical profession because that's normal, everybody's child engages with both of these services throughout their childhood, but social services? That's the big hurdle many families like ours struggle to overcome. There is a stigma, undoubtedly, and every time there is another heartbreaking child abuse scandal, social services get a bad press too. We assume Social Workers only get involved where there is major concern about a child being mistreated, and that when they arrive, their role is to bundle our children into the back of their car and drive away with them.

Until you have a child with disabilities, it's unlikely that you were even aware that every Social Services Department in the country has a team especially for families like ours. I would strongly suggest that you get in touch with them early on at least to make contact and get to know them, so that, if your family ever reaches a crisis point, they will be able to respond more quickly and in the way you need.

Every family with a child who has disabilities is entitled to a Social Services assessment, and you don't have to wait for someone to refer you, you can approach them directly. Think of them as the key-holder to all sorts of other services, they have to know about you and your family before they can open the doors to all sorts of things that really will help.

Following an assessment, you may be assigned a Social Worker, or you may be linked up with a Short Breaks Coordinator, depending on the complexity of your family situation. Additionally, you may also be allocated a Key Worker, who is one of the members of the multidisciplinary team working with your child. I never had one, but families I know who do feel very supported by these Key Workers. They will co-ordinate all the services and act as a sort of Project Manager for you and your child, joining everything up and chasing people on your behalf.

Short Breaks

Every child with a disability is eligible to "Short Breaks", which is the relatively new terminology for what used to be called "Respite", but with a complete shift in emphasis and the range of things available. The idea is that the whole family get a "Short Break", and unfortunately some of these breaks are very short indeed, around 2 hours for a play-scheme, which, if the parents have to take them and collect them, they will be hard-pushed to do much else during that time. However, the range of play and social opportunities available for your child is generally very impressive, and social services are providing really enjoyable regular experiences to suit all ages and abilities in the range of activities, social events and other things they are providing or commissioning.

Some families need much more than a couple of hours off here and there, and it is recognised that there are some children with complex needs whose parents need a complete break including regular overnight breaks. Toby fell into this category. Throughout his childhood, he would go and stay in a specialist, high quality children's respite facility for 3 days at a time every few weeks just so I could completely get my breath back. The quality of care he received there was outstanding, with all sorts of fun activities factored in too. He loved going, which makes it much easier for a parent, and I always felt that he was getting a very similar experience to a sleep-over that other children enjoy. He stayed at a local unit with 5 other children, a huge play-room, a sensory room, and staff that genuinely loved kids and being really silly with them. These staff were also highly trained, there was always a nurse on duty, and I could drive away completely unworried, and try and recharge my batteries, get the chores done that Toby's presence prevented, and most importantly, touch base and have fun with Francesca and Adam.

However, these residential Short Break facilities are falling out of favour with Social Services Departments because they are expensive. Fewer and fewer children are being referred to them, in fact most parents don't even know they exist. Instead, the trend seems to be to send a Care Assistant into your home overnight instead supposedly to allow you to have a good night's sleep.

An overnight carer in the home is simply not the same at all as having your child cared for in a highly resourced respite unit overnight. At home, it's hard to truly let go of your child's care, certainly emotionally. You can still hear your child's movements and noises, you can hear the care worker and how they are responding to your child, and you cannot switch off. Your child also knows that you are still in the house, and will be trying to attract your attention. Even with the most capable, competent and loving care worker in charge of your child's care, there is no way you can properly unwind, relax and recharge your batteries. Having someone in the house for any length of time also has a real impact on privacy, intrusiveness and your ability to talk freely and totally be yourself in your own home.

For families, respite units work really well for our children with complex needs in a way that can't be replaced by having an overnight carer in your house. However, for the local authority, it is a significantly cheaper option. My concern is that these well-resourced residential respite units are going to slowly disappear, one by one, from local authorities all around the country, and instead, families will be left with a half-baked, less effective but much cheaper option.

There is well-documented research which shows that children are better off in their own families than in the old-style institutions of several decades ago. The findings of this research are so obvious that they hardly needs stating; of course children are happier and better cared for by their loving parents at home than abandoned to be locked away long-term in isolated, bleak Victorian institutions.

However, this same research is now sometimes being used to justify the move away from the Short Break residential units towards the carer-in-the-home trend. There is no comparison whatsoever between the sort of cosy, homely respite centre that Toby loved so much and the old style institutions, and it's another example of how people manage to massage research to further their own ends, which are all too often financial ones. It's all baloney.

There is obviously a need for some children to be cared for overnight in their own homes. We had a lovely carer who spent every Monday night at our house for years. However, I think it is a very different service, and I would like to see parents making their feelings known loud and clear. The problem is that these residential care facilities are only intended for the most complex needs children in any Borough. In our Borough that was less than 40 families in total. These are the very families who are the most strung-out, exhausted and over-stretched, and too often, their voice just isn't loud enough, because there aren't enough of them and because they are too crushed to make any noise at all. These are the most vulnerable of families through absolutely no fault of their own, and it frightens me that the one resource that kept our family from completely collapsing under all the strain, the residential short break facility, could be quietly taken away.

Short Break funding covers a broad range of activities, and obviously there is a very limited budget. That's why a detailed Social Services Assessment is so important, so that this funding can be spent on families where the need is greatest.

However, don't be backwards in coming forwards when talking to Social Services. A lot of us have great difficulty telling it how it really is, because it can seem very disloyal to your child to spill the beans on all the negative aspects of their care. This is one area where it really does need to be laid on with a trowel, because otherwise, your child may not get their appropriate level of funding at all. That was something I was never all that good at doing, and I think a lot of parents struggle for exactly the same reasons. Every time I talk about my children I want to tell the world how fantastic they are, rather than focus on their negative aspects and needs.

Direct Payments

Social Services may decide that you and your child need an extra pair of hands, in the shape of a carer called a Personal Assistant, who is a paid carer for your child. In the vast majority of cases, this personal assistant will be funded through the Direct Payment scheme. Basically, you will be allocated a number of hours of care on a monthly basis, and then you will be given money to employ someone directly. Every three months the Council audits how much has been spent, and reclaims any surplus money. There are lots of checks and balances, you have to set up a separate bank account and use a payroll service provider that is approved by the Council, but effectively you are in charge. However, it all adds quite significantly to the already overstretched administrative burden that parents in our situation have to shoulder.

Direct Payments gives you a tremendous amount of freedom and flexibility to choose the right person to fit with your family, and to employ them for the hours that you most need, when you most need them. For instance, you can save up the hours and then employ the Personal Assistant for a long shift on a Saturday once a month to have a whole day off, or you could have them coming in for the busy two hours after school on certain days of the week on a regular basis. It is entirely up to you. It also means you can employ people you really know and trust, for instance very close friends or family members. That's allowable, as long as they aren't living in the same house as your child.

However, there are also downsides. Many families struggle to find a Personal Assistant at all, I've been in this situation with a vacancy for months. Meanwhile the council is being seen to be fulfilling their obligation by paying the money into your account, and you are left high and dry with no help at all. In the old days, each council would have employed a team of carers to send in to families on a needs basis, so they had to make sure there was someone there for you for the number of hours they had agreed to fund. It would have been untenable for a family to go without help for weeks on end. Operating on a wider scale, the council was able to offer these care workers a sufficient number of weekly working hours. Families trying to recruit care workers themselves don't have the large recruitment budgets enjoyed by the council for advertising vacancies, nor can they offer the sort of benefit package the council used to be able to offer their workers, but most of all, families struggle to find people able and willing to commit for a only a tiny handful of hours every week.

The other thing that the shift towards Direct Payments has changed is the employer's responsibilities. Sick pay, holiday pay, maternity pay, industrial accidents, grievance procedures, employment tribunals ..... anything that went wrong contractually used to be entirely the responsibility of the local council. Not anymore. Legally, your child is now the employer. If anything went wrong they would have to carry the can with only their family to support them, and there would be no help at all on offer from the well-oiled wheels of the council legal department. It's quite a scary thought, and one I think that simply doesn't occur to many of the families being put in this vulnerable legal situation.

Direct Payments has its advantages, but also comes with a significant potential risk, a lot of extra admin, and no guarantees that you will be able to find a suitable person to fulfill the role. This system is far from perfect, but more often than not, it's the only system on offer.

Other Social Services help

There are dozens of things our Social Worker has done for us, making our lives much easier and more manageable in the process. She was able to make referrals to various services, she was able to come to school meetings and support me in being able to voice concerns, she was able to kick-start the chain of events that eventually led to the council paying for a lot of building work around our house to make things more accessible for Toby. More than anything else, she was a very good listening ear, and an effective sounding board. I could ring her and talk things over until they were much clearer in my mind, and she knew and understood the dynamics of my family and what might work and what wouldn't.

The Local Parent's Forum

Social Services are head and shoulders above the other statutory services in that they will listen to parents and actively seek their involvement, and then try to shape services in the right direction. There is legislation that obliges every local authority to fund a Parent's Forum, which is the vehicle whereby parents of children with disabilities can engage with social services and help to direct policy.

It may be called something else in your area, but I would recommend that you find out what it is and join. In our area, the Parent's Forum has 900 families as members, and it runs training courses, coffee mornings, workshops, talks, so there are lots of opportunities to meet other parents and find out what's available for your child. Although it is funded by the council, it is run entirely by parents in our situation, and they work hard to find out the real areas of need and where gaps are in provision, and then they really set about making changes.

I know this because I became very active in our local Parent's Forum, and I was the Chair for a year, a year in which I worked harder, learnt more, and enjoyed more than probably any other single year ever. As well as a Chair, we had a Steering Group of about 15 members, and between us, we were invited to attend every local authority meeting concerning our children, taking our places as equal members with an equal voice, working alongside senior managers in all aspects of local children's services, as well as local councillors.

When I was Chair, I conducted a survey in our borough called "What Bothers You?" From that, we discovered that the four areas of most concern among parents were not the same areas that everyone had previously assumed were the big issues. There were certain parents with big voices who had campaigned very vocally about certain things, and the received wisdom had been that these were the areas that needed the most work. The results of the survey were quite a big surprise to everyone, and they were deemed as being, out of 50 possible areas, as follows, in order:-

Challenging Behaviour

Social Isolation of our Disabled Children

CAHMS provision

Therapy Provision, specifically Occupational Therapy and Speech and Language Therapy.

I held back the survey results until the day I knew that the Local Authority Cabinet Meeting was being held to discuss the austerity cuts for the next financial year. Every local authority in the country was having their budgets slashed by central government, and savings were going to have to be made across the board.

That day was one of my proudest moments ever – the stir that the What Bothers You Survey Report caused meant a total re-think around our local council's Cabinet Meeting table. Nearly all the services provided by the Council had their budgets slashed that day, but not the one parents like us relied on the most. The budget for disabled children's services was untouched.

Until then, I had never really believed in people being able to make a difference and being heard and listened to, but I do now. So, if you aren't 100% happy with the services being provided to your family and you think the authorities could and should do things better, there is a really effective way to get your views across and to be heard loud and clear. You don't have to go the whole hog and run the Forum yourself for a year like I did, just turn up at the occasional coffee morning, engage with the other members, and let people really know what bothers you.

If you can't get to the meetings or simply don't feel up to attending, there are other ways you can share your views. Many Parent Forums have a Facebook page and a website, and there may be other web-based or social media avenues open for you to voice your opinions.

The next area to really let people hear our voices has to be within the NHS and education. If only these organisations could learn to communicate in the same way as social services have learnt to engage with parents, everything for families like ours would become just that little bit better too.

TIPS, TRICKS AND STRATEGIES

Stay on side with Social Services, they can be really helpful and supportive.

Your social worker can advocate for you, refer you to other services, write letters to other statutory organisations in support of what you are trying to achieve for your child, and they can be there as a sounding board when you need to talk things through to get them clearer in your head.

However, always remember that there is a real conflict of interests going on, their objective is to protect their budgets, your objective is to get them to fund the things your child really needs.

Don't expect Social Services to tell you about every service they offer, your best source of information is always other parents.

Whatever they offer, take it, try it, you can always say that it's not working if it isn't appropriate later on.

Find out about your local Parent's Forum, the collective voice for all parents of children with disabilities in each area, and join them, and engage with them.

CHAPTER 15
Food Issues

All three of my children have struggled to eat properly. With Toby, it's fairly straightforward; his throat doesn't function properly, and after several years of being entirely fed by his gastrostomy tube which goes directly into his stomach, he is now learning to eat proper food. However, he cannot chew at all, and his swallow mechanism is still very poorly co-ordinated, so he can choke on clear fluid and lots of other food that the rest of us take for granted. There is a long list of forbidden foods including everyday basics like bread, cake and biscuits, any fruit that needs to be chewed or crunched, as well as rice and anything too stodgy. All his food has to be soft and mashed or pureed, and can't be either too runny or too solid.

When he was very little, we had a simply amazing dietician who looked after Toby's gastrostomy feeding regime. She warned me way back then that when there is a gastrostomy-fed child in the house, their brothers and sisters often develop eating disorders and food fads. I listened, took it on board, and then promptly forgot it.

Yet she was so right. At times, both Francesca and Adam's eating difficulties made Toby look like the most gifted eater on the planet, well certainly in my house.

In Francesca and Adam's case, being diagnosed with Obsessive Compulsive Disorder as well has led to some very interesting times, particularly in their early years.

Their OCDs were very different, but extreme food related issues were one aspect of this condition that they both had in common, and certainly the early years before we even knew of their diagnoses were very hard indeed.

For both of them there were enormous contamination issues, but it went much deeper than that. They both reacted very strongly and negatively to certain food tastes and textures, and trying to get them to try anything new was harder than getting them to pull their own teeth.

Over the years I developed a few strategies, some of which worked and some of which didn't, and then there were some that worked for a while and then just didn't anymore. When I found a food that they liked, in desperation I would give it to them so much that they ended up loathing it and then, that's it, it's off the agenda completely for the rest of their lives.

Adam was always far more difficult to feed than Francesca was. Looking back, I should have done things differently with Francesca. It was around the time of her seventh birthday that she announced that she was vegetarian and didn't like meat. I was completely strung out with Toby's medical regime, and Adam was a boisterous barely two year old. I just didn't feel at the time that I had the resources to indulge Francesca in what I felt was just a childish passing phase. Looking back, I should have taken her feelings much more seriously instead of trying to sweep them under the carpet. I kept up this battle of wits for several years, and I would turn a blind eye as Francesca exchanged the meat from her plate for Adam's vegetables, when I really should have just said, "OK darling, let's look at finding out how to cook some scrummy vegetarian dishes." So easy, isn't it, with hindsight?

Francesca was about 10 before I gave in and admitted defeat, and from that day forward her eating issues have slowly sorted themselves out. She had never enjoyed the processed quick-fix nursery type food like chicken nuggets and sausages, and soon she was eating a healthier diet than most children of her age, full of a wide variety of fruit and vegetables, any cheese she could lay her hands on, rice, pasta, eggs, and fish like it was going out of fashion.

With Adam, mealtimes were becoming increasingly more stressful. I was having to find inventive ways of negotiating with him to eat virtually every mouthful of food. He had an extreme dislike of every single vegetable, apart from broccoli and cucumber. He also developed huge fears about contamination, and soon a long list of environmental conditions had to be adhered to before he could agree to let anything pass his lips.

When Adam was 12 he lost 20% of his body weight in less than four months because he could hardly bring himself to eat anything at all. It is the scariest thing to watch a relatively healthy lad fade away in front of your very eyes, and the more I coaxed and cajoled, the less keen he was to try and eat anything.

This wasn't anorexia; this was a total fear of food causing him harm.

In the previous few years I had grown accustomed to producing several dinners in quick succession for him, sometimes as many as 6 or 7 in one evening, and one after the other they would be left uneaten and then scraped into the bin. It was sheer terror on Adam's part. If the cucumber was touching the chicken nuggets there would be cross-contamination and he couldn't eat it. If there was the tiniest microscopic speck of dust barely visible to the human eye, it too had to go in the bin. I had to prepare food without breathing on it ....he would stand and watch me make him a sandwich while I held my breath the whole time. Sandwiches couldn't ever have more than one ingredient in them. Any sort of sloppy food that mixes ingredients too was a complete no-no. So stews and casseroles were completely off the agenda.

With Adam, I noticed that he had some funny little ways about food almost immediately he was weaned onto solids as a very small baby. He simply would not tolerate mashed potato. He would hold it in his mouth, with his mouth shut tight, and not make a sound for hours on end, looking very sad and forlorn the whole time. He simply refused to either swallow it, or let me take it out of his mouth. The only way to resolve the situation was to hold his nose so that he had to open his mouth to breathe, and I had to have the other hand ready to scoop the mashed potato out of his mouth in that nanosecond his mouth stayed open. If it hadn't been so sad it could have been quite hilarious.

I would leave it a few months and try again. Mashed potato just happens to be one of my favourite foods on the whole planet, and I just couldn't understand what there was not to like about it. I tried everything, even flavouring it with chocolate or using food-colouring to disguise it by turning it bright blue, but the harder I tried, the more he resisted.

It still didn't sink in that this might be serious, or ring alarm bells when that lovely dietician warned me about what may well lay ahead.

As far as food was concerned, Francesca had the best possible start in life. When she was very little, she was my one and only, and I wanted to do everything completely correctly. She only ate home-made food from the best ingredients. I had read a little article about giving babies drinks of the water that vegetables have been cooked in as long as you never add salt to the cooking, so from 6 weeks old I would religiously save all the cooking water from spinach, broccoli, sprouts and cauliflower, keep it in the fridge, then warm it up later and give it to her in a bottle, as an extra to her ordinary baby milk. So as her taste-buds were forming, she was experiencing a wide variety of vegetables. It's probably no coincidence that from her earliest years she has simply adored vegetables of any shape, colour or description.

When Adam was a similar age, we were living at Guys, and he was weaned entirely on ready-made shop-bought jars of baby food, since there wasn't any other way of doing it at the time.

Adam in time started taking his contamination issues to yet further extremes. If someone upstairs had the audacity to cough during the whole time his meal was being prepared then he simply couldn't eat it. Then he couldn't bear that I touched his food, so we commenced an 8 year period when I had to wear not only disposable gloves whenever cooking but a shower cap as well. I drew the line and flatly refused to go as far as a face mask too. It was only just over a year ago when I went bald during chemo that the shower-cap requirement was lifted, and less than a couple of months ago when I quietly stopped wearing disposable gloves.

Adam also still struggles to try anything new whatsoever. As he gets older, he is working hard to overcome his food issues and will sometimes gingerly sample something new. Recently, he discovered that tomatoes aren't actually all that bad, and will now eat them sometimes, but he remains largely the meat king of the household.

Cooking smells affect him badly too, due to his sensory sensitivities. If something has been cooked that has left a lingering smell he finds unpleasant, then he cannot eat even his favourite foods.

Basically, every mealtime I end up cooking three entirely separate meals, one for each of the children, but there are still no guarantees that everything will get eaten. Adam will push his food around his plate some evenings, and not be able to say why he can't eat it. Now he's older, he will try to tell me he isn't hungry because he doesn't want to cause me any extra bother, but more often than not he will admit that he is hungry around 11pm so on many nights I'm still cooking a second meal for him at nearly midnight.

If it was solely up to Adam he would simply live on 6 or 7 bowls of Coco Pops every single day. He can eat them till the cows come home. Francesca would be very happy to survive on chocolate, cheese and vegetables. One thing they will both eat is ice-cream, but the only flavour they have in common is Ben & Jerry's Cookie Dough. Nothing plain, cheap and simple food-wise in our house.

It's also difficult with drinks. Adam spent several years when he could only drink fizzy drinks and only out of individual bottles. Normally only Dr Pepper or Lucozade, but occasionally Powerade too, and he would always insist of sticking to the same flavour of that. Again it cost me a fortune, but he simply didn't feel safe in drinking from cups because they might have got dusty in the cupboard.

You have to find a way to help your children eat, and I battled with this one for a very long time before I mastered some strategies that have been particularly helpful with Adam, slowly also trying to extend the range of foods that he is willing to try.

The most important strategy was to try and understand why he felt like he did about food, which in turn helped me to become much less stressed and worked-up about it and to remove as much of the emotion as possible away from mealtimes.

Adam is extremely sensory sensitive, which means that all his senses are far more acute than most other people, and he doesn't have the ability to tune them out when necessary. When you are over-sensitive to food, a texture or a taste that feels wrong in your mouth is so overwhelming that it feels like physical pain. So these children try to protect themselves from further pain by only sticking with a very limited range of food that they know they can tolerate.

Add in to the mix their intense feelings of guilt when they think that their mum is upset or cross about their behaviour. They don't understand that their whole mouth-feel experience is different from that of other people. They see other children eating reasonably normally, and so they start to believe that they are being naughty, a feeling that is reinforced when they see exasperation etched all over their parent's faces.

Factor in, too, how mothers react emotionally to food. They place enormous value on their role in nurturing their offspring safely to adulthood, and being able to successfully feed them is part and parcel of the emotional baggage that comes with being a mother. This is a universal truth the world over, and mothers also use food-based treats such as sweets or biscuits as a reward. The natural assumption is that mother cooks, child eats, child grows healthy, bigger and stronger, and mother feels great pride about her maternal abilities. As mothers particularly, we tend to judge ourselves and others on our ability to feed our children, and when this natural process is interrupted in some way we feel a huge sense of failure and disappointment. We also pick up disapproval from family and friends when they see our children refusing food time and time again. Sometimes this disapproval is unspoken, but very often people are openly critical about your parenting skills, saying things along the lines of "Well my kids just have to eat what they're given and that's that", or "I think you need professional help for your kids or they're going to become anorexic", or "Just let them go hungry then."

I've had all this unsolicited advice plus lots more, and it really isn't helpful. If I had children who didn't have the sensory and other problems mine have, they would eat for me too. If the answers were really as simplistic as some other people think, we'd have sorted all these issues out much much sooner.

One of the most damaging things about all this unsolicited advice and implied criticism is that the kids hear it too, and it makes them feel absolutely awful about themselves. Kids who have eating problems very quickly pick up on all the signals of disapproval, and they can develop feelings of intense guilt and self-hatred as a result.

Going to friend's houses often becomes a big issue. Other parents usually want to feed visiting children, and that can cause tremendous stress and upset, not just to the children who have food issues, but also to the other set of parents who sometimes take it personally that a child will not eat their food.

On top of this were Adam's contamination issues. When a child won't eat because they perceive a plate to be dirty, it's very easy for a parent to feel that they are being criticised and to take it personally and become defensive. I've learned the hard way that remonstrating with your child is a complete waste of time, and only serves to increase the heightened sense of negative emotions.

I've learned that negative emotions have to be separated somehow from mealtimes, and the most important strategy I developed was to find ways to remove emotional flashpoints related to eating. The second most important strategy was to try and truly develop a sense of understanding as to where Adam was coming from with his food issues and why.

One of the easiest and simplest of the strategies I implemented fairly early on was to buy Adam his very own personal supply of cutlery and cups and then store them separately from the main kitchen things. He has his own tin for cutlery and his own kitchen cupboard for cups and cereal bowls. This has helped Adam in particular, and he will now drink copious amounts of milk from his own stock of cups so he isn't so reliant on unhealthy, bottled fizzy drinks.

I had to accept that mealtimes resembled a battleground. I was always holding my breath and hoping he would eat something without rejecting it. I began to realise that when your child rejects your food it actually feels as if they are also rejecting your love and you as their mother. So, without realising it, a cloak of anticipatory stress was already hanging low over the dining table before I'd even called the children in to eat.

I had to take a long, hard look at how emotions were further complicating an already difficult situation. My anxiety about whether they were about to eat or not got translated into their heads that they were upsetting me. They would be frightened, not just of the food itself but also of having to deal with the emotional fallout of my possible disappointment. So I knew I would have to take a very different approach, and that started with me having to examine my own emotional relationship with food and any related beliefs and values concerning feeding my kids.

Once I'd analysed my own emotions and pre-conceived ideas, I was then able to start thinking about how to create a totally non-threatening environment at mealtimes.

The first thing was to make sure Adam continued to eat enough to keep him at a reasonable weight, but in a way that was both low-key and unemotionally-charged. Balanced diets and getting a whole range of nutrients could wait for the time being. I decided not to push him into eating at all, but to build on what he liked and felt safe with. I also didn't let him know that I was changing tactics, I just did it.

I went shopping and filled the food cupboards and fridge with lots of Adam's favourite foods. An hour or so before a mealtime was due, I encouraged him to snack on whatever he fancied, then if he managed to eat enough of whatever he wanted at his own pace, the pressure was off and it just didn't matter if he didn't eat a formal meal.

Basically I was doing exactly the opposite of what I and thousands of other parents normally do. I had always strongly discouraged snacking between meals, and particularly within the hour or so before a meal would be due.

For the next few days, Adam survived mainly on eating Coco Pops but he was also grazing on cucumber, grapes, sausage rolls, a particular type of processed cheese and the one brand of yoghurt he enjoyed. I also relaxed the family mealtime rules – he was allowed to eat wherever he felt most comfortable, sometimes that was on the sofa in front of the TV, other times he took his food up to his bedroom. Anything to just reduce the pressure, while putting him firmly in the driving seat and allowing him to slowly begin to form a more positive relationship with food on his own terms.

This regime continued for several weeks, but slowly mealtimes became much more relaxed and non-contentious. That's when I was able to begin to make other small changes.

I tried to introduce an element of fun. Adam has always enjoyed science at school, so I implemented laboratory-style food taste tests in our kitchen. I used a tea towel to blindfold him, I gave him a "spit-out" bowl, but the rule was he had to keep each of the taster tests in his mouth while I slowly counted to ten. We livened it up and made it ridiculously silly, with me adopting the persona of an over-the-top bossy mad scientist, and sometimes Adam couldn't eat simply because he was laughing too much. I also structured the tests in an informal way, and he had to decide whether food was sweet or savoury and if he recognised the taste. I would ask him to try and describe the texture. This had the added benefit of distracting him away from focusing on the overwhelming sensations in his mouth that caused such a negative reaction.

Each taste test would have ten tastes, about half-and-half between foods I knew he had tried before and liked, and new foods he had never sampled previously.

Encouragingly, at most sessions there were one or two completely new tastes that were acceptable to him, and over the next few weeks I was able to introduce a fairly wide new repertoire to his previously very limited food list. Among these new foods were prawns, crab sticks, gnocchi and bananas, plus several others too.

The secret was to make it fun, and to be very silly while we were doing the tests. A short while afterwards, I also introduced the idea of cooking something brand new that he had never tasted before, which we nicknamed "Mummy's mistakes". If he didn't like them at the very first tentative microscopic sample, then without any fuss whatsoever, it went straight into the bin. I always remembered to congratulate him on at least being prepared to try something completely new, and then I would cook something else from the very safe and established original food list.

Basically, food will always be an issue, and something that Adam may always struggle with, to some extent. However it doesn't have to be a drama anymore. After all the years of stress and worry, we can actually laugh about some of the food issues now too.

It's a tough thing to let go of all your preconceived ideas and allow your standards to drop in terms of things like eating at the dining table, but the payoff has been so worth it.

TIPS, TRICKS AND STRATEGIES

Make mealtimes enjoyable, not a battleground.

To do that, you will probably have to take a long, hard and painful look at your own relationship with food, and examine your own values about mealtimes.

Try and work out what food-related behaviours from your children trigger an emotional reaction in you, and then try and work out why.

Never force-feed or stand over them until they have a "clean plate".

Try and ascertain the difference between a very real food issue and what is actually a control issue, remembering that control issues work both ways – you may be trying to control your child by insisting they eat everything you put in front of them just as much as your child may be trying to control you or their environment by refusing to eat certain things.

Either way, do whatever it takes to remove or reduce conflict. It's not about either you or your child standing their ground and winning, it's about finding a way to help your child develop a positive attitude towards food, and if that means you have to step back and "give in", then so be it.

Give some thought as to what may be causing the food aversions. If there are also tactile aversions to the way certain clothes feel, coupled with strong aversions to certain smells, it may be a sensory sensitivity issue, which needs to be investigated because it may otherwise impact negatively on many other aspects of your child's life.

If they just can't stand the taste or texture of pasta, for example, it's just not worth the fight. Give them potatoes, rice or bread instead at mealtimes, and try them on pasta again in six month's time.

All behaviours, including food-related ones, are a form of communication. What is your child trying to tell you? Use your instincts, it could be anything from toothache, to a loathing of a particular food, to not having many friends at school, with a 101 other possible explanations in between.

Separate out other feelings that you associate with food. If you've slaved lovingly over a hot stove for several hours to produce a nice meal for your child and then they won't eat it, they are not telling you that they don't love you or appreciate your efforts, they are just telling you that they don't feel able to eat it.

Be prepared to do fun deals with your child, and if they will try something they don't think they like then so will you. Be brave and let them spoon-feed something you really don't like. Be careful though, I was happy to tell my children I didn't like beetroot or raw carrot, but I would never have been able to go through with eating something that I really felt strongly averse towards, such as snails or offal!

Try and notice the positives, and acknowledge them with praise, even if they really are tiny, baby steps.

Never show anger or disappointment during meal times – even if you have to force it, look happy around them when they're eating, to reinforce the concept that eating is an enjoyable experience.

Lower your standards for a time if it means they'll eat better. A happy child stuffing their face whilst sitting on their bed playing a computer game at the same time is a much better result than a tearful, resentful child refusing to eat at a formal mealtime sitting around the dining table.

If all else fails, or even if it doesn't, try and find a funny side to the whole mealtime rigmarole, and make sure you and your child can laugh about it sometimes.

CHAPTER 16
Meltdowns

So what exactly is a meltdown? I'd been dealing with them at home for many years before I actually knew the answer to that one.

I've mentioned in previous chapters the concept of sensory sensitivities. Before we can really understand meltdowns, we need to understand how a child who is overly responsive to all their senses can become completely overloaded and overwhelmed by too much sensory information flooding into their brains simultaneously.

Imagine that all your senses are super-sensitive. Your hearing is so acute you can hear the tiniest of sounds coming from the house next door or footsteps on the pavement outside a hundred yards away. On top of this you don't have the ability to filter out unwanted sounds and just focus on one sound. For example, if you are watching TV a plane may fly overhead but you are normally barely, if at all, aware of it because your attention and hearing is focused on the TV. You may also be vaguely aware of children playing in the garden next door, but again, because you're watching TV you hardly register their howls of laughter.

Someone with sensory sensitivities is unable to filter out the peripheral, unimportant noises, so that the plane and the children in the garden are competing for their attention in an equal way to the programme that they are watching on TV.

However, it isn't just that your hearing is super-sensitive, it's all your other senses as well. Colours are brighter, contrasts are sharper, and the carpet that lies between where you're sitting and the TV is taking as much of your attention as the TV itself. You are acutely aware of where the seams of your clothes lie across your skin, and certain fabrics feel incredibly rough and uncomfortable. Your sense of smell is also able to detect smells that others wouldn't notice, so you can smell the cooking from next door's kitchen as well as the bitter smell of tarmac being laid on a nearby road. You can even still taste the dinner you ate two hours ago as if it were still in your mouth.

This overload of sensory information is continually flooding your brain, clamouring for you to process it all the time. It becomes exhausting and your ability to concentrate on the TV, or anything else, is severely reduced which is really frustrating. Some of this is information you may find extremely unpleasant, such as the jet noise from the plane, the white noise from household appliances, the busy pattern of the carpet or the horrible smell of the tarmac, so unpleasant that it almost feels like pain.

Your brain is having to work overtime all the time, and there isn't much spare capacity for it to take on much more. Then something else happens, something that really upsets you, a sudden power cut perhaps so that the TV programme you had been trying to watch is no longer on the screen.

Your brain simply can't process any more, you are overloaded already, and it feels like every part of your being is in pain and the only possible direction you can go towards emotionally is a meltdown, an explosive total loss of control.

Watching a child have a meltdown is really frightening, because it becomes very apparent very quickly that this loss of control is beyond your reach, and the child is no longer aware of time, place, danger, or anything whatsoever. They may be lashing out, or shouting, or throwing things, or throwing themselves around violently, or banging their own head against the wall, or conversely they may withdraw so deeply into themselves that it looks like they have gone into some sort of shutdown and they are no longer responsive.

To the uninitiated, it can sometimes look like an extreme temper tantrum, but the causes, the feelings and the manifestations of the behaviour are completely different. In even the most dramatic of temper tantrums, the child maintains at least some level of self-control, and tantruming children normally have enough self-awareness to protect themselves against injury. Not so with the child in the middle of a meltdown.

So what can you do to help your child through the meltdown, and out the other side as safely and as quickly as possible?

There are lots of strategies you can use, but the most important thing to remember is to stay very calm, very quiet and gentle, and very non-confrontational.

A parent's instinct when their child is unhappy is to rush in and try and comfort them with lots of affectionate kind words and gestures. It took me a long time to understand that often this is exactly the wrong thing to do.

This child is reacting in this way because their senses are already completely overloaded. Talking to them or hugging them will add yet more sensory information to process, making them worse not better. The one thing that will escalate things even further is to use a tone of voice that sounds scolding or angry. Sitting here writing this down, it is so flipping obvious, but when you have a full-blown meltdown unfolding in front of you and it's putting everyone in the room at risk of injury, it can be very difficult to modulate your voice so that it sounds calm and unfazed.

I have two ways of dealing with this. Firstly, I say absolutely nothing at all. Anyone who knows me for the chatterbox I am will find that very hard to believe, and yes, it is so against my nature that it is almost impossible. Secondly, I sing. Either songs that Toby really responds well to and likes, or I just sing what I would normally want to be saying but to a made-up tune.

The one thing of paramount importance is to do anything you can to reduce the risk of injury. So any sharp or heavy objects need to be removed from the area as quickly as possible, and you also need to encourage other people to move away too, although you can enlist their help to move possibly dangerous items into another room out of harm's way.

If your child is likely to be throwing themselves around and at risk of hurting themselves, some level of restraint may be your next and only option.

If at all possible, attempt restraint from behind them so that you are not at risk of being hit or kicked. One way of restraint that can also help to restore calm to their being is to use a blanket or large towel and wrap it right around their body from behind. In some situations this can have a pretty instant, calming effect, some children find being wrapped in a blanket immensely soothing, and you can actually buy specially weighted blankets online especially for this purpose.

If you don't have a blanket or towel to hand, or you have tried it on previous attempts and you know that your child reacts negatively to it, then just try and hold them from behind so that at least they can't use their arms to injure themselves or you. Again, remember to stay completely calm, and to project to your child a sense that you are in control, so that they feel that you are solid, stable, calm and safe.

Are you able to work out what the trigger was that caused the meltdown, the final straw that sent your child over the edge? If so, how easy is it to fix and can you do it single-handedly? If there are other people in the house and you have managed to successfully contain the situation for a minute or two, can they help?

When a child is in a meltdown, they have such strength that holding them still is exhausting, and depending on how big they are, it might prove impossible to do it for more than a very short time.

Distraction can occasionally work very well in bringing a child out of a meltdown. Sometimes I have just started to make some silly noises, or to laugh loudly like I'm cackling, or to walk away from holding Toby but far enough away to be out of his immediate reach, then I do a really silly clown-type dance. It doesn't always work, but sometimes it has an instantaneous effect at calming him down, and maybe even making him laugh.

Another little trick we've discovered almost by accident that works extremely well with Toby is to make a big flamboyant gesture before tipping a huge bag of brightly coloured socks all over the place. Toby has immediately calmed down, sat himself on the floor, and spent the next hour or so methodically trying one sock after another on his hand and closely peering at the shape his hand makes inside each sock.

Once Toby is out of a meltdown, there is often a recurrence almost immediately, and he can spend the next two to three hours going in and out of the meltdown state, so that things can still be quite fraught for a significant length of time.

If nothing is working at all and you aren't strong enough to hold your child safely to protect them from injuring themselves or others, you may have no alternative but to remove any obvious danger, and then leave them alone in a room while you try and get help. I know of some parents who have been left with no other option but to dial 999 for the police. It's not an easy thing to do, and it is very much a last resort, but if there is no other way to help your child through this, that may be the only thing you can do to bring it to a close without anyone, including you and your child, getting hurt.

If meltdowns are a frequent occurrence, it would help if you can get some professional help, but that can take a long time to access via CAMHS, and even then the help may not be easily forthcoming. It can also help to let social services and your child's school know how you are struggling. They may be able to help you access other services or put you in touch with other organisations that may help in the meantime.

There are dozens of books on the market that can also help you develop coping strategies and maybe some basic, low level interventions that may make a difference. The internet, too, is full of information, and can help put you in touch with other parents who are coping with similar levels of meltdown.

Often it is parents themselves, by pooling our combined knowledge and experience, who can help us find our own ways forward. Somehow you will find a way to help your child cope better, but you may have to search high and low to find the right answers. Whatever it takes, it will be worth it.

Remember too, the phrase I kept hearing, that all behaviour is a form of communication. Your child is trying to tell you something, and you will find the right way to respond to them eventually.

TIPS, TRICKS AND STRATEGIES

Stay calm, keep any stressful tones out of your voice, and project relaxed body-language.

Give your child space, don't crowd them or make them feel pressured in any way.

Remember, they can't help this behaviour.

Prevent injury in any way you can.

Avoid standing directly in front of them, because you may be putting yourself at a greater risk of injury if they kick or lash out.

Get help if you need it, if possible have a planned strategy for getting help quickly in these situations.

Keep a diary of when these things happen, what your child was doing immediately beforehand, who was in the house, and what the emotional atmosphere was generally at the onset of the meltdown. Over time, if you can identify triggers, there may be things you can do to remove or reduce these triggers.

Sing instead of talking. It will ensure that there are no negative tones in your voice, and it may reach a different part of your child's brain and help them connect with you more quickly, enabling them to come out of the meltdown sooner.

Some children respond well to having large earphones placed over their ears during a meltdown, some don't. What works for one may escalate the meltdown in others.

Others respond well to being wrapped in a comforting or weighted blanket, but again, others might not.

Distraction can also work well – doing something funny or ridiculous like jumping off the sofa or laughing your head off maniacally may just surprise them out the the meltdown. Experiment with different silly things you can do.

Reduce as much sensory stimulation as possible, including refraining from hugging them.

Don't try to reason with them, tell them off, or let them see how upset you are finding their meltdown. They are beyond overload already. They cannot take on board any more input, particularly verbal communication, and they are not able to cope with their own emotions right now, so they really mustn't be burdened by your own emotional state. Stay calm, and be as emotionally neutral as you can possibly manage.

CHAPTER 17
And finally

Phew – I've actually written my first ever book! If you're still with me and have read it all the way through, very many thanks.

I hope you may have learnt something, or at the very least enjoyed some of the stories and laughed a bit along the way.

It's been great fun writing, as well as frustrating, unsettling, exhausting and crazy at times as well. I've been surprised at how revisiting some of our family's past has opened up all sorts of old wounds and within seconds, I've sometimes been transported back as though it was all happening only a few minutes ago. There have been some quite difficult bits with the occasional raw nerve twanged as I wrote, but overall, I think it's been very cathartic, and has helped me make a bit more sense of some of the rather surreal things I've gone through with the children.

I really hope that other parents whose children are at a different stage to mine may take something from this book. I don't have all the answers, and I often made it up as I went along. The Tips, Tricks and Strategies might not all be exactly right for you and your family, but I hope you can make up some of your own that work for you. I also hope it makes you feel as if you aren't quite so alone; for me sometimes the sense of isolation was the hardest part.

A handful of very trusted individuals read the early drafts of this book, and their input and comments have been invaluable. Among them were a doctor, a senior social worker, and an experienced teacher. Their feedback was very positive, and some felt they had learnt things and would be taking a different approach in certain areas as a result of things they had discovered from the book. I really hadn't expected that at all; I thought I was writing a book specifically for parents in my sort of situation.

So, it would be great if this book is also read by professionals, and I hope that they, too, might learn something from it, although I think some may find it very tough-going and a very difficult read. Sadly, it's often the professionals who didn't need to read the book in the first place, the ones who instinctively "get it", who may be most affected by this book. They are the ones who are sensitive, committed and among those who will always be remembered with great fondness by the families they work with. Unfortunately, it's likely to be the ones who could really learn from it that won't believe that it applies to them.

I have tried to be fair, and I hope I've been balanced in praising the good as well as highlighting the less good. Overall, the people we have met along the way have been fantastically supportive on an individual basis, but there is something about the endless meetings and their dynamics that make even the best, most "on-side" professional behave differently in a group setting, and that has sometimes been very difficult to cope with.

What's next for me? Well a long sleep, loads of TV to catch up on, and friends to invite round for dinner, then back to the writing. Most of my friends and family are surprised that this book isn't about cancer, and I'm being urged to write my next one about getting through the last couple of years of chemotherapy, surgery and everything else.

As I was writing, I realised this book wouldn't even be needed if only the organisations who work with our families could slightly shift their thinking, working culture and focus in just three key areas. It would cost very little, and actually save money.

1. Partnership working If all professionals could be given the tools, the confidence and the encouragement to work in partnership with parents, acknowledging them and their ability to take part in the decision-making processes as an equally respected member of the multi-disciplinary team, outcomes would significantly improve immediately. It would also markedly cut costs because, with the the parents on board, who know their children best, there would be a better chance of doing things right the first time around. Additionally, when people work together there is more trust and collaboration, which in turn reduces stress on all sides.

2. Empathy Putting the emotional, practical and physical needs of people back in the heart of all practice, and ahead of the processes and systems which have dominated our statutory services for far too long. Empathy, in an environment of partnership working, can go both ways and can be mutually empowering. Just as it is important for families, it's equally important for staff, because they can't run on empty either. Basically, empathy lets people know that they actually matter, that they are valued and accepted, and quite frankly, we can't put a price on that, yet it costs absolutely nothing.

3. Simplicity It's back to those systems and processes again; everything has become far too complicated, far too many reports, regulations, tick-boxes, meetings and forms at the expense of time to really care. Of course there must be record-keeping, but we passed the tipping point a long time ago when the sheer volume of administration ceased to be in place for the benefit of the children and their families, it's now acting as a barrier to having the time to properly care in a meaningful way. The onerous burden on professionals is taking its toll in stress and burn-out. Most of the paperwork is now for the benefit of the insurance companies, the lawyers or for Government statistics. It's not there so that a better level of service can be delivered. It's all so counter-productive too; a lot of the admin is there on a "just-in-case-something-goes-wrong" basis, yet while backs are turned and their paperwork is being completed, the scope for things to go wrong is massively increased.

These are low-cost or no-cost solutions where everyone would benefit, most of all our children. I'm convinced that if we could somehow work together to bridge the divide between families and professionals so that we're all working together with humanity and kindness right back in the heart of our society, we could use all our physical, emotional and financial resources much more wisely.

Due to my cancer, I don't know how long I have left, but one thing I do know is that I want to spend as much time as I possibly can in helping organisations make these changes. I speak at conferences, seminars and other events, and I also facilitate workshops to help professionals and parents explore better ways of working that will benefit everyone, particularly our children. This is about working together to make things better for everyone. If you'd like me to work with your team, organisation or parent group, please get in contact so that I can help.

There are lots of ways you can get in touch –

Through my website	www.yvonnenewbold.com
Through my Facebook page	The Special Parent's Handbook Facebook Page
You can follow me on Twitter	@SpParentsHbook
Or via Linkedin	uk.linkedin.com/in/yvonnenewbold/

TIPS, TRICKS AND STRATEGIES

We've come to the last section of these, so this final selection is aimed at you moving forward with your family, and having the confidence to do it in whatever way suits you all best.

Always trust your instincts, because you're much better at this than you think you are.

Don't be afraid to do your own thing, to think outside the box, re-invent the wheel and to do whatever it takes to get you all through things.

This book is about how I did things, you have to work out how you'll do things, but always give yourself permission to do it your own way and to make it up as you go along.

Find something to laugh about every single day.

Find something to be happy about every day too.

Everything will work out far better than you ever thought possible. Believe in yourself and your children, take it one day at a time, and have as much fun as you can, whenever you can.